DEDICATION

This is dedicated to the loving family and friends I'm so blessed to have around me. Each of you has been so instrumental in supporting me and making all this possible. To Veronica, my loving wife…You inspire me. How many individuals are blessed to work with someone they cherish as much as I do you? To Natalie and George and my brand new grandson Logan – You are the next generations. It is for the next generations that wake me up in the morning with the word "strive" in my blood. This book is also dedicated to my good friend Martin Rosato. You are always my family and the greatest mentor I've been blessed to know. Each of you has made this book possible. I thank each of you.

TABLE OF CONTENTS

Acknowledgments

Surprisingly (or not), the typical result one can expect to achieve is nothing…
Let me repeat that to you…Your results if you are typical will be dismal.

Interestingly and tragically, the "typical" reader will never get to the end of this book. And by the way, if you are "typical", I bid you farewell and adieu. Please go on to the next "next fix". Sooner or later you will learn… or quite possibly you won't. And at that point you may change careers or move on to working in some else's practice. Either way, it's totally okay. You see, I realized some time ago that about 60 or 70 percent of the population are dabblers. Dabblers earn nothing, zero, nada, zip. No income...and perhaps a loss of income? Typical people do nothing and usually always achieve nothing. If you are atypical… if you have the attitude of "can do" and put your money where your mouth is, please read on. Do something. Implement something. If it doesn't work; make a change…and implement that. Try again…keep trying. Try again if that didn't work. Guess what? If that result didn't happen try again. Persist. Eventually you will find that breakthrough. Honestly and in my experience, as I kept trying and trying and failing and failing, eventually as I made that transformation – that breakthrough – it was so much sweeter knowing the path I had to take to get to it. It was earned!!!

INTRODUCTION

I want to start off by saying you are about to read a book about online marketing. Since an eBook, a Kindle edition and especially a physical book will be around forever, does it even make sense to discuss online marketing since it's ever-changing and dynamic?

Although I realize that yes, online marketing is fluid and things do change, there are tried and true principles that never change. In fact, many of these principles will undoubtedly increase in effectiveness as the web continues to grow and traditional advertising fades away.

This book has the best of both worlds.

What you find inside are the principles that will work...when you implement them. They are based on the rock-solid strategies that we have been using with our clients for years. The results speak for themselves. One piece of advice: use the resources. They will help you get more patients and more freedom.

On that note, the difference between average practices and truly *great* practices comes down to implementation. Often, the one thing that differentiates one from the other is how successful new ideas and strategies are implemented. The same is true for the information in this book. It works, and similarly, it only works when implemented. You *knowing* all of this information won't help you make any more money or sell your services or even your practice for more. When you *implement,* this information can make you an additional mid to high six figures or even seven figures annually, PLUS you will help and heal more people, create a more stable practice, and really feel a sense of accomplishment from the efforts and results you have obtained.

One of the most common questions we get from a medical practitioner is, "How am I supposed to get all of this done?"

The answer is that you now can or you will be able to soon, know how to build (or find) good teams. Toward the end of the book, I have included a section on where and how to find competent people to help you implement your web strategy.

Are you excited? If so, then let's get started!

CHAPTER ONE
PATIENTS FOREVER: DOING ALL THE RIGHT THINGS AT THE RIGHT TIME

Congratulations! Imagine yourself a year from now and five years from now. Begin with the End in Mind, right? Steven Covey listed this as the first rule in his book The Seven Habits of Highly Effective People.

So how does that equate in your world? Imagine you have successfully developed your practice to its fullest potential. What does that look like? Are you clear? Are you clearly articulating your vision to see that? Do you have your practice goals written out? In my experience, most practitioners don't. Why? Well, most won't take the necessary actions for true success. Simply stated, the business drivers that contribute to creating a successful practice have changed drastically in the past ten to fifteen years. In the realm of marketing, that change is much more dramatic. Consider if you will the "clutter factor". Chet Holmes coined the term before his untimely passing in 2012. I worked with Chet and respect greatly the legacy he has created and the impact he has had on the world of marketing and sales and developing business acumen in general. According to Chet, the clutter factor is the single greatest marketing challenge each of us face with our marketing programs and initiatives. In 1992 the average consumer was exposed to 3,000 commercial messages per day...in 2012 the number increased tenfold to 30,000. That number staggered me and seemed somewhat unrealistic. So I went to Google. They cite many references that give numbers. For example: "**The average American is exposed to 247 commercial messages each day." Consumer Reports Website.** And then the numbers sort of went haywire, if you will. The various sources they reference give numbers of: 247, 600, 3,000, 850, 3,000, 3,000, 600, 500-1,000, 2,500, 1,500, 3,000, 3,000, 1,600, 3,000, 3,000 and 1,500 respectively. None of these numbers were even close to Chet's. So I'll summarize by saying who cares! Whatever the number is one conclusion emerges. There is a tremendous amount of other practitioners out there vying for the attention of YOUR future patients. How do you plan to "pierce through" this clutter factor with YOUR message? That's probably one of the most important questions you should be asking yourself.

Here's part of the answer. You may think your web presence may not help you that much. People know you or know of you. You and your team (team, not staff!) ask for and are referred to future patients. And you would like to believe you are earning enough business.

I will ask you another important question. How much of your current revenue from new patients came from online...whether from a search engine, Google AdWords, or your website? How many people are actually searching for a practitioner like you anyway?

The majority of your potential patients are; that's who!

Research shows that, increasingly, fulfillment of online searches is done overwhelmingly by local businesses. A 2010 study by BIA/Kelsey and research firm ComStat found that 97% of consumers research their purchases and local services online before they ever do business with a local company - this included medical practices. According to another *source* listed in the graph below, the number is somewhat less – around 82%. Both numbers are equally impactful.

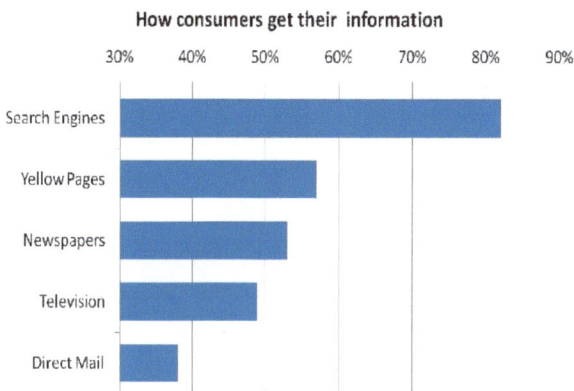

How consumers get their information

	30%	40%	50%	60%	70%	80%	90%

- Search Engines
- Yellow Pages
- Newspapers
- Television
- Direct Mail

Source: Webvisible and Nielsen, reported by Marketing Charts- 2009

One more stat I want to throw at you. According to Entrepreneur Magazine, the average annual sales of small businesses in the US are $3.6 Million. It is $5.3 Million for those with a website (2010).

Perhaps fortunately for you, most practices aren't focused enough on developing their online presence. Obviously, if your future patients are researching online (and they are) and you don't pop up when they research, you stand a great chance of not earning their business...plain and simple.

This is a dangerous spot to be in. Technology always changes. Advancements are always right around the corner. Whether or not you change with it is a decision. If you fail to adapt to advancement in technology, you either make that decision consciously (insanity!) or you fail to realize you've even made a decision (unconsciously incompetent). Examine your own habits and validate what I just said. Traditional media is declining. The days of strictly advertising with yellow pages, newspapers, television, billboards and radio are over. It's a new day dawning. Technology and the mechanisms with which we communicate are constantly changing. The strategist adapts. The strategist *anticipates.* The graph on the following page illustrates my point.

Percent of Businesses Using Digital and Traditional Media in their marketing budgets

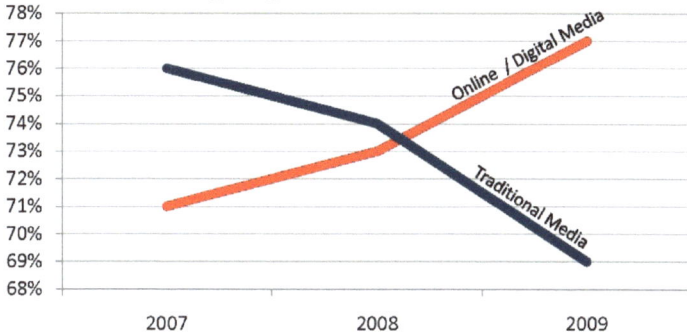

Source: The Kelsey Group August 2(

Think about it. How often do you use the Yellow Pages or open an encyclopedia to research? The majority of the human race now relies on Google for these types of things, don't we? What amazes me is the amount of businesses I run across that have the print version of the Yellow Pages still in their budget. I've seen budgets of $20,000 or more allocated to Yellow Page advertising. I seriously think this is a profit leak. Let me ask you a question. How much of your marketing do you truly track? If I were to sit down with you and analyze each of the areas that you have delineated as marketing (yellow pages, newspaper ads, radio, TV, billboards, etc.) could you provide me a monthly flash report? The report you provided me should indicate your return on investment itemized for each category in your marketing plan. Could you do it?

I really have yet to see any practice that produces this to the standard where it's useful. Yet, when I develop this set of Key Performance Indicators in "getting the business" - also known as marketing and sales- I usually find that traditional offline marketing doesn't produce a rate of return anywhere near what your online focus can...if and only if done correctly, with piercing effectiveness.

What that means for you

What is your online focus? How do you corner your market? Do you buy into the myth that you can't "own" the highest search engine rankings on the Internet? Can a local practice even compete in this ferocious online arena?

As it turns out, they can. In 2013 Google completely changed the rules of the game with the introduction of "Panda" and "Penguin". I promise not to get too technical. Google made some of the most significant changes to their search algorithm that determines how websites get ranked. The great news for the local practitioner is that they've shifted searches for brick & mortar businesses to something called "local search return" or specifically Google Places / Google + Local, a feature that used to be only available on their Google Maps service.

So what exactly is the local search return? As originally designed, when a user searched Google Maps, local businesses would appear in the geographic area that was being searched. If a user searched "Orlando, FL", for example, the Google interactive map provided helpful markers placed around the map, indicating local businesses (that subscribed) that were nearby. Not surprisingly both eating establishments and hotels were the first type of businesses to recognize this value and use it. Eventually other business types recognized the value of this.

When first introduced, Google's regular search box was only returning lists of links as search results; they weren't map-based and often weren't nearly as useful as the map results that Google Maps was returning. Consequently, Google transitioned the local search returns into their regular search page. Now when you search for a physically located business, the search provides a mapped location as well. This is great news for local businesses! The deck has been "unstacked". There is now a real opportunity for competition. It's very realistic to now actually have an opportunity for your practice to show up ranked in the top spots for the best search terms.

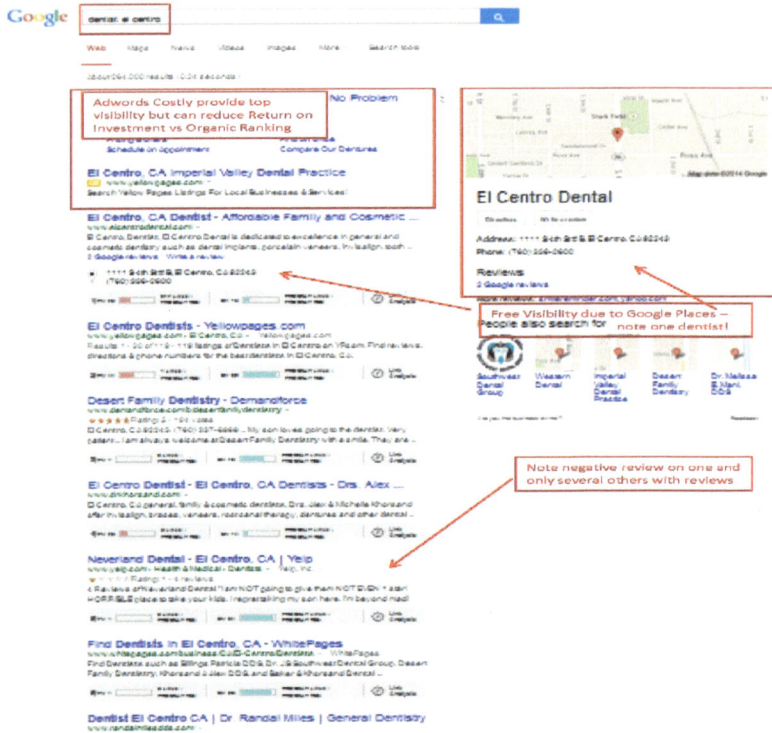

The screenshot above shows how powerful that local search return

feature is. Prior to Google making these changes, your chances of

competing on popular search terms was practically zero. Now every

local practitioner has a strategic opportunity to rank high for local

searches in their area. Granted, this is "smart work". Obviously there

are plenty of your competitors vying for these key words and these top

spots. Here's a takeaway for you. Just having a glorified brochure of a

website up and several keywords optimized on each page of your site

isn't going to get you far (dare I say "recipe for disaster")

There is a process, however, and if you do a good job, are careful, and follow all the instructions in this book you can get first page rankings on your local search for good keywords.

WARNING

I mentioned just now that Google updated its search algorithm. Be very careful to avoid any duplication of content! For example, a practitioner with two offices may decide to duplicate some of the pages because the services are basically the same. Google of course won't recognize that you are the owner of both locations and sites; so you'll be harshly penalized. The great news is that Google has particularly focused on rewarding main street businesses that offer quality content. Consequently, they are punishing so called "black hat" search engine optimization techniques including fake backlinks, fake listings and duplicate content. These actions can get you delisted from Google's search index entirely, and possibly forever! Though this may seem kind of harsh, but remember that Google's efforts to clean up its search engine will benefit those of us that play by the rules. In fact, we hope they go after the scammers and spammers so that real businesses that Offer value and quality can rank well so that they are easily found by those who are the top to people who are genuinely looking for information, help and service.

Caution! Run as fast you can from anyone or any company that tells you this process is easy! It's not. If you are told it's as simple as keyword selection, purchasing ghost written content and submitting it to blogs and other sites, they're misguiding you. It's usually always the case that the content purchased in this manner is rewritten by software, rehashed and possibly word for word duplicated material. It's quite possible you could get penalized as mentioned earlier. You may find that your outcome was to gain ground or far surpass your competitors, when in fact you're losing ground.

Good quality content is the key to online success. It always has been and probably always will be. Many experts will tell you that it does take time… and they may be right. I think it may be smart to rethink this whole strategy of content. Why not just outsource it? Unless you or a member of your team is really good with content, why in the world would you not outsource it?   In either case, you have to ensure there are both a creation process and a review process in place. Both will help your chances of first place ranking on optimal keywords.

Predictably, many try to game the system with duplicate content and "black hat" link strategies. Yet Google is definitely on top of it and at this point you would be hard pressed to find a high ranking site using these tactics.   Still, there are many less reputable and over promising companies offering the "easy" way to first page ranking. Beware. Confirm, don't just ask, whether their content is duplicated,

THE WAY I SEE IT:

- Your web presence is no longer optional. More and more, people are using it to find businesses and needs (statement of the obvious)

- Local Search is the big player now in Internet marketing. You need to make sure your page ranks high in the list of results when users search!

- Be very careful of how you enter the search engine market! A substandard presence online can be worse than no presence at all

- If you need help, make sure to choose your marketers carefully! Some may attempt underhanded tricks to boost you in the search rankings (like duplicate content) but these tricks can often carry with them severe penalty from the search engines for trying to game the system!

CHAPTER TWO
FLASHY WEBSITES WILL KILL YOUR MARKETING: THE CHANGING OF THE GUARD

The first chapter you just read through made it abundantly clear how important Google is. We also examined how Google's local search returns, and ranking in general, are extremely important to your marketing efforts. We know that traditional media is fading fast, and if you want to stay on top of the game you're going to have to get into this search business right away!

The natural next step would be to go and get ranked, and for that you need a website. Your website is as much a part of this process as anything else, and if you're going to get good conversions from your search rankings you need a functional website that fully caters to both the needs of your business and the needs of your patients.

The creation of the website can be a minefield, especially in today's whiz-bang, Flash-enabled, Web 2.0 world where everyone thinks every website needs interactive menus, drop-down interfaces, and all other sorts of bells and whistles. You see it all the time, in fact, people ask for "Web 2.0" or "interactive" developers, or developers will try to push Flash this or Web 2.0 that on you, saying how important it is and how professional it makes your site look. You may be tempted to believe it. The truth, however, is this: for most small businesses and conversion rates, all of that fancy stuff does not matter. A solid, simple website will work far better at increasing your conversion and getting customers to contact you. This may seem counter-intuitive, especially in a world that seems to value style over substance, but it's true: simpler pages have, in our experience, been far more effective at getting customers to call or email you than other flashier pages.

This will seem a little daunting, especially considering how much we've been talking about the importance of getting listed properly. And that still holds true: getting ranked high on Google still matters the most. In fact, the rest of the book after this chapter is devoted to that very concept. The website, however, is an integral part of the chain. It's by no means the most important link in the chain, not by far; it needs to be done well, however, or it has the potential to ruin the entire concept of getting ranked on Google. The bottom line is this: if your prospective patient does not actually pick up the phone and call, all that effort you put in into getting visitors to your site will have been wasted. No matter how flashy and fancy your website is, if there are no conversions, then that website was a waste of money, simply stated.

So what is an Effective Site? What's the Secret Formula?

Based on what I just said, your site needs to prompt your visitor to get into action. That usually means they pick up the phone and call for an appointment. But, what if your visitor is not ready to make an appointment? In a moment, I'll discuss the mechanics of what your site needs. Yet I believe it is more important to expand on your visitors who are not in "buying mode" and are not ready to book a time with you. It's critical that you understand the buying pyramid. The pyramid and ideas contained therein are also courtesy of Chet Holmes.

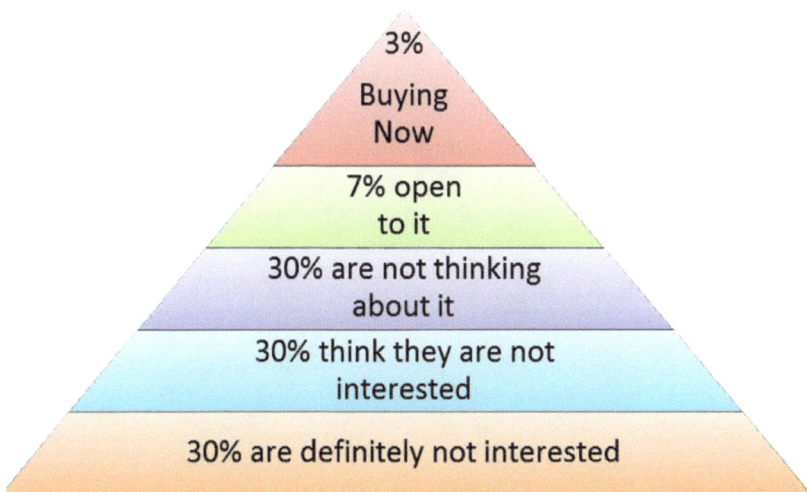

3%
Buying
Now

7% open
to it

30% are not thinking
about it

30% think they are not
interested

30% are definitely not interested

As Illustrated on the previous page, there is always a very small

percentage of a buying audience who are buying now. This is for any

normal product or service where there is a usual supply and demand.

That would definitely include most medical and dental practices. The

3% are in the market.

For a dentist, those buying now may have a toothache and are definitely

buying now. There are 7% who are open to it. They may be dissatisfied

in some small way with their current provider and so they are open to

your message. The next 30 % are not thinking about it. They are not

against it, or for it...they just aren't thinking about it. The next 30%, as

you can see, think they're not interested. They are not neutral like the

30% who are not thinking about. And finally, there are approximately

30% who are definitely not interested in your message. In the dentist

example, their brother may be a dentist and so they would definitely

not be interested in you. It is an interesting fact that most advertising

focuses on the 3% that are buying now and the 7% who are open to it.

Most marketers won't take the time to educate the other 60% who are

in the open to it and not thinking about it categories. This is 60% of your potential buying audience! I think it's a huge waste of marketing spend to inform those that are buying now about your latest equipment and the fact that you're the best in town (which may or may not be true). First of all, if they are buying now, they may have already been checking around for the best solution. You may have to "reengineer" their buying criteria around your offering! This is usually a losing battle because someone else (usually your competitor, right?) has developed the buying criteria around their offering. Would it not be easier and cheaper if you can engineer the buying criteria by educating your patient first on what it is?

Since we know that most new patient relationships being with an online search, let's discuss what you should be doing with your site once they get there.

<u>What Should Your Overall Site Look Like?</u>

In general, there is a rule that can be applied to any medical office trying to optimize their local search return...less is more! Solid, functional sites with a call to action will be far more effective for you than a glorified online brochure. I recommend your layout be this simple:

- Home page

- Blog

- About Us / Services

- Contact Us (with map and phone)

The end, that's it.

It might seem a bit *underwhelming* to you, and sparser than all of your competitor's websites. Those website are not ours. Your website is designed for conversion, not oohs and aahs.

I discussed calls to action above. Each of your pages should have one. A call to action prompts your prospective patient to do something. Usually that something is to call you or email you. I will discuss this later in the follow-up section. For now, just know that I recommend a call to action such as "click here for an appointment" on every page and that your phone number be prominently displayed "above the fold" (the viewing area on your site that doesn't require scrolling down). Studies indicate that at least in western society, our eyes gravitate toward the right side of a page. This is how Google designs their AdWords. I always recommend a form be added on the home page to opt in for a special report particularly developed for the search term that page is geared towards. This is an example on the next page:

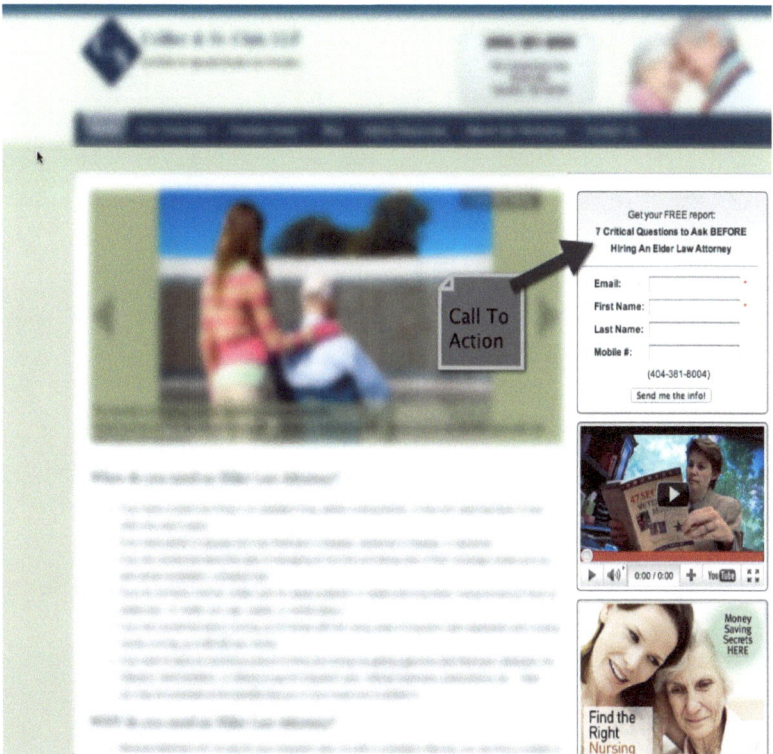

All practices would be well advised to add an upcoming events page and provide press releases about your practice.

When discussing website appearance, the mantra of first impressions could never be truer.   You have about 3 seconds to capture a visitor's attention or they're gone. When a visitor arrives, they visually scan your

site and need to instantly understand what you do and how to take

action. Below is a before and after case study using a "heat map". Heat

maps show scattered eye movement that bounce all over the page. It's

what each of us does whenever we view material.

This is a screen shot of the home page for this company. The goal is to

get the viewer to recognize instantly the turquoise button.

This next photograph is of a heat map that shows scattered eye movement s (yellow lines) that bounce all over the page. Drawn by bright blocks of color and sharp areas of contrast, the eyes do not find a place to settle.

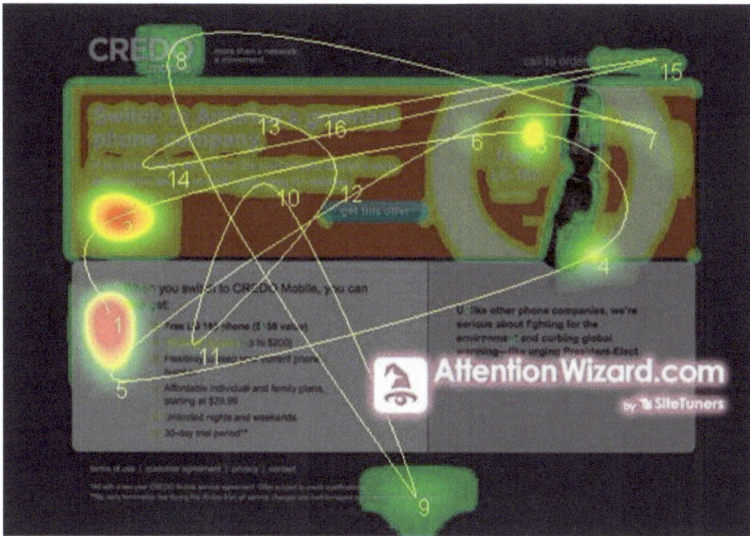

This was observed in practically all the participants! As you can see the call to action button is practically invisible to the participants.

This is the redesigned page. Notice for yourself where your eye focuses

More than likely, your eyes focused on the product first and then the

call to action.   This is clearly intentional.   At least in the western

hemisphere, we tend to focus immediately and primarily on the left side

of the page.

The final heat map shows the eyes are attracted to the cell phone, and the call to action button. This new page had a 58% improvement in conversions with this change. Obviously, this was the intention.

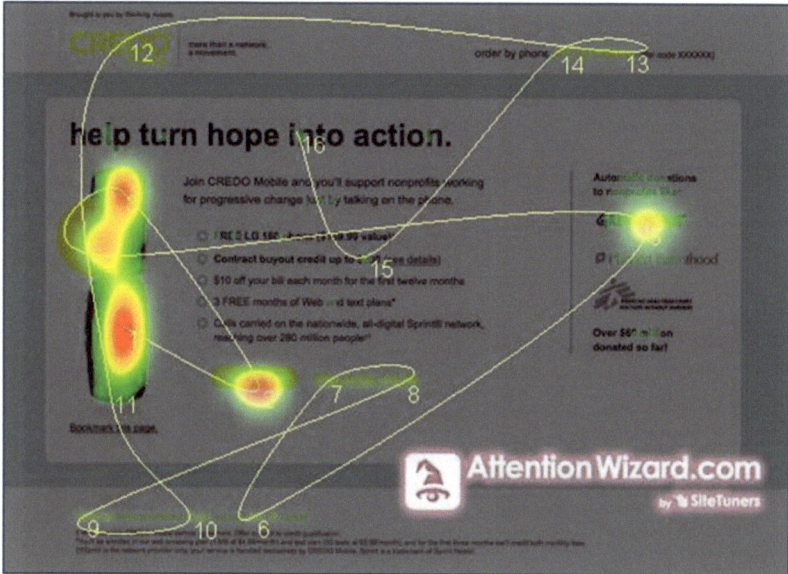

The Psychology of Color

Let's discuss color. Most website owners leave it to chance. They assume their designer knows what they're doing. They may, but again why leave it to chance? Every detail is critical – including the choice of color.

According to the Institute for Color Research, over 60% of the initial impression of your site is based on color alone! Color psychology is a powerful workhorse in the area of influence. The use of specific colors can trigger emotional responses based on nationality, past experiences and even personal preference.

For example, red, orange and yellow colors all emit excitement and surprise. The use of these colors draws the eyes and so are effective

attention grabbers. Call to Action buttons are frequently done in these colors. Caution is in order though not to overuse these colors. Their purpose is to stand out and therefore your viewer's eyes will be drawn to it. Too many sites will overuse these colors. Again, be very judicious in the use of these colors. Just like using too many exclamation points, your viewer will tire easily if subjected to the overuse of these colors in your material.

Purple, blue and green are soothing and calm colors. Use these colors to deemphasize or soothe your visitors.

This is a visual representation of many of the colors and their use.

Here's the breakdown of each page.

Home Page

This is the most important page as it connects your audience with the rest of your site. But it's important for this page to connect your reader with the rest of the site. Make sure the page is easy on the eyes, has a blurb about you, and invites the reader to explore more of the site. Above all, however, make absolutely sure that the home page features the blog prominently or at the very least provides a link to your blog page!

YouTube is now the second most visited site in the world after Google. The world is in love with video. Should you not incorporate this in every conceivable fashion in your marketing deployment initiative?   Studies show that you can expect a minimum 30% increase in conversions when your viewer can watch a video of something related to your practice on your homepage. I recommend you incorporate a small, short (90 seconds – 2 minutes) video on your home page.

The next piece I am discussing is critically important: Take a look at your copy if you have an existing site. Is your content focused on your latest and greatest? Is it focused on the fact you are the top practitioner in your area? That you have won numerous awards and are well respected in the community? I hope not. I trust since you're reading this that you have recognized that each of us want to know how <u>we</u> can benefit. So here's what your copy should include:

1. The benefits you provide someone (not your services or 'features') but the actual benefits patients achieve as a result of working with you.

2. Information about what is on your blog and links / enticements to good blog posts

3. Call to action – what are you providing in order to induce your future patient to call or provide you with their contact information. Can you provide special offers, special reports, checklists, etc.?

These 3 items are so important to your success that we usually always write these sections for our clients and develop our client's follow up process around them.

Blog

Blogs have now been around for at least twenty years. Never underestimate their effectiveness. They have withstood the test of time for a number of years. Your blog provides the following key success factors:

First, this is your chance to shine by developing your online persona. You have the opportunity to craft your message about the latest and greatest...whatever that is in your specialty. This is how you become an author/expert. Granted, it's the first step of many, but your outcome is to be perceived (because you are) as THE authority. Obviously, you will discuss new developments in your specific specialty that affects your patients. You can also link out to a few recent news articles and provide some commentary about how they affect your readers. I have observed and recommended to my clients that discussing local information is a gold mine. Granted, the majority of your readers may gloss over this because the content may not be relevant to why they are on your website. Yet, the fact you discuss the local scene/current events can't help but boost your rankings with the various search engines. Think about this: YOU are a member of the community. Are you involved? Think about the opportunity to sponsor in some small or large way, various marathons, 5ks, festivals, or parades coming up. Write a few paragraphs and include links to all the details in one place. If you know that parking is tough for these events, provide information about other parking; if there's a booth at the festival not to be missed, then tell your readers about that. You will be surprised that these will become your most popular blog posts. It also builds up your credibility as someone who lives, works, and cares about your community.

The most important thing a blog provides for you is a conduit for the search engines to find new and relevant content - If it happens to be about your practice, so much the better.   It makes sense that by talking about your specialty you will very naturally use the keywords that you are also optimizing. Simply stated, make it a rule to write about stuff you know about and that provides value to your readers. However, try to keep it simple and try to write on a level that will capture your reader. Many practitioners habitually speak in their own language of medical terminology.

It's proven that consistent blogging is important for not only ranking, but for keeping your reader engaged. Yet, it's my experience that you probably won't develop the habit – if you are like most of my clients. I understand taking time out of your week to write two or three blogs is difficult. I understand you're busy. We made the decision to do all of the writing for our clients. We hired awesome copywriters and pay them well. Clients get good content several times per week...and they don't have to do any of the work.

Video Blogging: Video blogging is a great way to add variety and increase your audience. I mentioned YouTube a few paragraph earlier and its status is a testament of how popular video is. Including video on your blog may help you appeal to a new audience.

Video blogging (or Vlogging) can open up a whole new set of possibilities in addition to attracting new visitors. Some things are just easier to explain with video. Discussing the proper way to brush teeth is a perfect example of a topic that is just easier to grasp with a visual demonstration of what that looks like – rather than reading about it.

Not all kinds of video will work on all kinds of blogs: some subjects lend themselves to video blogging, but for other subjects, you may struggle to think of appropriate video ideas. Lastly, because video lacks text, it traditionally had been tricky to optimize a site or post with video content. I will discuss later several breakthroughs we have that takes both your video content and a transcript of the blog you recorded and distributes it instantly to hundreds of social media, indexing, blogging and other sites.

By adding video to your blog you really have a way to stand out in the crowd. What better way for your potential patient to get to know you than to have the experience of listening and watching you discuss the things you are passionate about.

About Us

In my experience, the about us page is usually always wasted real estate. This page is the most visited other than the home page, statistically. Most site owners completely miss the opportunity to connect with their visitor on this page. If you sample several of these pages on any random site, you will usually find a blurb about the practitioners and perhaps a map and hours of operation, etc. Is this helping drive conversions? It's probably not. Your readers may care about your years of experience, but it probably won't be the driver that gets them to book an appointment. The point is that most of the sites out there never give the visitor a reason to do business with them.

I am going to suggest a different tact. What if you made the About Us page, actually about them – your patients? What do I mean by this? Why don't you take the information about you and position it as a benefit that your patient receives. I'll give you an example.

Dr Jones recently developed a series of special reports that holds promise for back pain sufferers everywhere. Discover a new technique you can do just 10 minutes a day that can eliminate pain completely. Obviously, I made this up but you get the point. I understand that medical practitioners have to be careful with this from the standpoint of exaggerated claims. Yet, we want to answer the question your prospect may need to know. Why should they trust you with their health versus your competitor? If you continue to ply information at them about you, your practice and why you're different you are actually doing exactly what every other practice is doing. Remember earlier I said that we want to engineer the buying criteria around what we deliver. Your site had better deliver on that ability.

Contact Us

The Contact Us page should be very simple. You should have your email, your phone number, and a map to your business. That's it. You can perhaps put a slightly different or stronger call to action on this page, but for the most part this page should be clean, simple, and not distract the reader from picking up the phone or opting in to your newsletter. Some add a contact form on this page. That's perfectly fine and it's a great idea. Yet the most important thing is to provide a clear phone number or email that is directed and answered by an actual human.

Call to Action

I have outlined the layout. Let's now discuss your call to action.

What exactly is the criterion that comprises an effective call to action? What specifically should you have on your site to generate conversion – meaning your visitor is now in process with you?

An effective call to action is one that makes your prospect pick up the phone and call right away, or one that compels them to provide you their email. It's critically important that your call to action be very strong and that you have built sufficient credibility. Why? Because, wouldn't you agree that most of us are inundated with too many emails? Remember the clutter factor we discussed earlier.

A "must" for you is offering a special deal for those prospects that provides their information. It could be a discount on a service? However, I'm not a believer in discounting services. Thankfully a time tested better way is to provide something ground breaking in the way of a special report that you know your audience will find valuable. For example, The Five Most Critical Questions you should Ask Before Plastic Surgery. You can target it even more by making it local. For example, The Three Things You Must Know Before Seeing Your Chiropractor in Phoenix. The information could be just the thing a prospective patient needed at the right time. So they will take action by opting in to your report.

This content is so important that we usually write this report for our clients and place it on their website (after their review, of course). The titles above take a "consumer advocacy" approach, which we've found attracts a lot more clients than traditional advertising.

We also typically recommend that you not just ask for their email, but for their cell phone number as well. People are giving out their cell phone numbers quite readily now, more so than a few years ago, where it was very difficult to get someone's mobile number. Many people nowadays use cell phones as their primary or even only phone number, and thus they're more willing to give it out to people who ask if the reason is compelling enough.

If you follow all these steps, anyone who signs up their email or phone number will be a "warm" lead. A "warm" lead is someone who's going to be very receptive to your business and much easier to convert into a client, since they've showed a great deal of interest in your services—they've pretty much done the hard part, which is getting in contact. You have to act on this, however; warm leads, like anything else warm, tend to cool over time, and if you don't act quickly it'll be that much harder to seal the deal. This leads us to our next item of interest: follow-up systems!

Make certain you have a follow-up system in place so that you can call a lead within five minutes of them entering a form. Yup, I said five minutes! If you can get them within 5 minutes, you know they're an extremely warm lead; you know they were on the website, you know they were interested, and you know they're looking for you. This is a very warm lead and much more so than someone who just happened to see your name in a direct mail piece or in a local flyer!

CHAPTER THREE
SEARCH TERMS ARE UNDER RATED

What good is a website if no one visits? The search engines need to find you first for anything else to happen. In order to rank high you have to use targeted keywords. I promise this is not going to be a complicated discussion. Yet, it's critically important that you and I discuss it.

Most people understand the concept of keywords. These are the words (either one word or multiple words) that users type into a search engine. The search engine will return the best search results for the specific phrase the user entered.

Our company Breakthrough Strategies does a lot of our client's online marketing for them. The subject of keywords is usually the most difficult to discuss. I can't tell you how many times I have had a client excited as they notice they are in the first position on Google. We find out that they are specifically searching for their practice name! I almost hate to tell them that practically no one is searching for their exact name. If they are then it means they already know of them.

You're online to get new patients who are trying to solve a problem that you can solve; in short, you need to present an attractive solution to people with problems. People need help with "cavities", "tummy tuck", "backache relief", "hearing aids"; these are the keywords people are searching for. Very few are typing in your practice name. They are looking for the things that you do.

Another mistake I constantly see is the use of jargon and industry specific keywords. Example: how many are searching for "myocardial infarction prevention"? You would be better to optimize a page on your site (more about this later) for "heart attack prevention Sacramento" (if you work in Sacramento obviously). Google provides data about what people are searching on. Quite possibly, the searcher in this example was typing "how to prevent a second heart attack. The lesson is to always examine the keyword selection from the point of view of the searcher.

This is one of the biggest pitfalls I see with most businesses. They make the mistake of not defining where their traffic is coming from. Specifically, the knowledge of what people are searching for. There are a number of tools that can make this process easier. You just need to decide if you can expertly deploy it insourced or whether you need an expert to execute it.

The other pitfall that practitioners make is they typically want a neat, catchy name or their business name in the URL. If you want to rank really well, you're going to have to make your URL keyword rich.

Here's an example: Let's say you're an eye doctor in Dallas, Texas, and you've decided on the keyword phrase "color contacts Dallas TX". A great URL for your website, then, would be "http://www.colorcontactsdallas.com". This will help tremendously in your efforts to rank high on Google. I realize that that's not a pretty name, and if you want to have your business name website URL for business cards and marketing materials you still can: It's very inexpensive to have multiple domain names, and you can easily have your webmaster redirect "http://www.johnsonandsmithllc.com" to "http://www.colorcontactsdallas.com" and still reap the benefits of the keyword-rich URL while having a professional URL on your business cards.

A keyword-rich URL is one of the first things you can do to influence your Google search rankings. I will discuss other methods to rocket you to the top, of course, but if you start this process without a keyword-rich URL, it's going to be a very steep uphill battle. Do yourself a favor and start with a keyword-rich URL- it's very helpful and makes everything that comes next way easier!

Niche Segmenting

Something else you need to think about is niche marketing. As you may have guessed from that specific URL, you can't be highly ranked in everything. Unless you're a general practice in some discipline in a small town, more than likely there will be a ton of other practices vying for that top spot in different keywords and you're going to want to select some specialty or niche to focus on.

This isn't to say that you can't do other things or cross-sell once you're in front of your patient, but you definitely have to put some thought into your niche strategy. Where is most of your revenue coming from? Ideally where do you want it to come from? What's the most profitable part of your practice?

What it comes down to is this: To dominate online, you have to know where you want to go and focus on one thing. Find something that you'd be happy with if the majority of your business came from that one thing. It's there that you're going to want to focus your keywords. Now please don't misunderstand the context of what I just wrote. I didn't say that you needed to only focus on this always. Just right now. While you're building your online dominance you want to pick your battles carefully. Why spread yourself thin at first? Why not focus on where you really nail it? So my advice logically is to focus on the service or product where your highest profit margin is. For example, if you're an acupuncturist I would obviously recommend that we dominate the keyword "pain management". We would make a keyword-rich URL out of that keyword-rich phrase, and then proceed to dominate the search rankings focusing on that.

Once we've narrowed down between 3-5 keyword phrases with a few words in them each, we will want to make sure those keyword phrases are in your title tag in your website and that title tag starts ALWAYS with those keywords. You want the title tag to start with the keywords, move into the location, and end with the business name. Don't lead with your business name- the business name will come along for the ride. It's all over your website, and people (and Google) aren't going to miss it. Start instead with the important keywords, and make sure those are peppered all throughout your site.

WARNING

Don't overdo it! Google is looking for real people with real content, and not automatons who simply spew out keywords nonstop. There's a joke in the Search Engine Optimization world about this:

Q: How many Search Engine experts does it take to change a light bulb?

A: Light. Bulb. Lamp. Fluorescent. Incandescent. LED, Flashlight...

The joke is light-hearted, but the message is clear: don't over-saturate! We will want to make sure your keywords as a percentage of total content average around four percent. This is an optimal percentage for keywords to words. I know I said I would not become too technical and I broke my promise! I guess the point is that your content should be written in a natural way. The search engines, including Google, use algorithms that can decipher when real content are being distributed to real people and when it is prepared and distributed for an audience of one...the search engine. If the folks at Google believe you're trying to game the system, they have in place processes to penalize your site.

I may also suggest another strategy initially as naturally several competitors are already optimized for the optimal keyword phrases of your area of specialty. Why not focus on smaller subsets of that keyword phrase: the logic is if you can dominate two or three smaller keyword phrases, you may receive more traffic and end up actually getting more business than the your competitor that just went after that larger, broader term.

Those are, in effect, the two separate strategies you have to look at from an inside perspective. All of the concepts discussed thus far are important to understand from the standpoint of either doing it yourself, or arming yourself with the knowledge when dealing with marketing companies

JUST THE FACTS

- Keywords are important; don't bother with trying to rank for your business name. Rank with keywords that get traffic and are terms that ordinary users are searching for!

- Incorporate your keywords into your website, and make sure your internal or external webmaster forwards a professional-looking URL to the keyword rich one!

- Specialize, specialize, and specialize: don't go for the broad market. Find your most important profit center and focus on it for your initial online initiative.

- Leverage your marketing tools, especially the people around you: they are, for the most part, representative of your clients and can offer insight into how your clients would search for you.

- Be natural! The search engines penalize keyword stuffing; Avoid a keyword density of over 4% at all cost. Just write naturally, and you can assure you will have a sufficient amount of keyword density with a natural reading flow.

Chapter FOUR
GOING LOCAL: IS BLOGGING DEAD? NAILING IT WITH ADVANCED TECHNIQUES FOR LOCAL

Okay, so this is where we are so far. Whether or not you have implemented so far (hint) you've got a good handle on website design, the use of colors, placement, your content and a good basic primer on SEO. I hope you're asking "What's next?" You may also be thinking about adding a Google Places / Google + Local page. Should you do it right away? Should you expect your site's ranking to go off the charts soon thereafter? If you said "hell yes" or some other really positive affirmation, then I like your style. But hold on for a minute please. I have to get you grounded with the reality that you site may still have a long way to go. In this chapter, I will help you figure out how to make your local business big-time online using several advanced local search techniques!

Blogging

Google has said emphatically that they're going to give stronger credit to resources that are both relevant to the user and current. This makes sense, given the overall makeup of the web: new content ages quickly, and very often more timely information is far more useful to an online search than older. You can address this by adding new content to static web pages, but this method is time-consuming and more trouble than it's worth. The solution? Blogging. It is true that blogging has become the online activity-du-jour on the Internet—it seems that everyone and their cat have one, and sometimes several. The fact of the matter is, however, that blogging has become a powerful force. It also has one distinct advantage for us: It is by far the easiest, most convenient, and most effective way to add new, updated content to your website. It's not necessary to change your site around at all. Your designer should empower you so that regular blog updates can be seamlessly added without the need for his/her involvement.

It's especially helpful when you consider Google's other preference in high-ranking Google search results: steady, relevant content. There's no "magic bullet" or fast-track way to rank high on Google. Honest and truly, slow and steady wins the race. So if you think about it, blogging is absolutely, positively 100% all about this. Blogging is essentially your branding. It's an expression of your practice culture. It's the opportunity to reach your intended audience with your message. Always, it's a way to connect with your audience.

Is there a right amount of blogs? It depends. Are you blogging for the sake of that audience of one – Google, or are you speaking directly to your patients, both present and future (and what about past)? From the discussion so far, I want you to keep Google in the back of your mind and focus primarily on the audience you want coming in your front door. In other words, keep it real. I want you to put yourself in the position of your client. Would you want to hear from your dentist three times a week? How about your chiropractor? Probably not right? Here's the issue: in my opinion too many practices project the same message type continuously. How many times a week or a month should the receiver of your message have to hear about your latest and greatest gizmo that may as well cure cancer? Yes, I'm a little on the facetious side, but is this not too far off from real life. Here's a pointed question. How large is your team? When they were hired did you place any value or even ask about their ability to communicate? Not just internally with patients and the organization, but written word. Unfortunately most practices and I would place the number at over 90%, do not look to their staff as a resource for marketing and positioning the practice in the community. Really, what I'm trying to say is why don't more practices create a blogging team? Everyone has a different job in your practice right? Each has a valuable contribution for blog content. I find that all too often, most of the clients I work with put walls up with job descriptions. "He's in the front office, what could he add of value to a blog?" I want you to think about all the different topics that come up in the front office. This person, for example, may develop a blog article about the top 5 issues your patient face with insurance acceptance of _____procedure and how they can better prepare in advance. I know everyone's busy. I and my team have worked with various types of medical and dental practices to understand this concern. I also know where there's a will there's a way. If you've really got a team member that has the talent, you could also pay them a bonus per blog. You could also outsource it couldn't you?

What is the ideal and what is the minimum amount of blog posts you should be putting out each week? Because of Google's preference for updated, steady content, you should be blogging at the very least once per week, and each blog post should be between about 250-800 words; they can be longer but they don't need to be, and they definitely shouldn't be any shorter than 250 words or Google may regard them as sparse on content and less valuable.

This may seem daunting to many, and understandably so; the thought of composing another written piece every week isn't appealing to many folks out there. If you truly think about it, however, once a week isn't too bad; that's only four times a month, and if you make a schedule and stick to it you'll find that blogging really isn't the chore you thought it would be.

If you're finding that you have time for more, it's beneficial to increase your frequency to twice a week; my experience tells me this is optimal. I don't advise to go over that. In this case, more is not necessarily better. Some think that twice a week is better than one, and then five times weekly must be better than once weekly. I can guarantee you will actually hurt your ranking. The algorithm Google utilizes can calculate when the posts are created for Google and when they are created for the end user's consumption.

Blog Subjects

It should go without saying that your blog should be useful, current and relevant. Here are the three main content points you should be hitting in your blog posts:

1) Talk about What You Do

This one may seem pretty obvious, but it's worth mentioning: talk about what you do and what the benefits are to your patients, not who you are. Don't talk about yourself, how long your practice has been around or how great your service is. This won't help you. It doesn't help you with the search engines and more importantly, it won't help you with you patients.

For example, let's say you're practice attracts a lot of military and a new law or change happened in VA benefits regulation. A perfect blog post would be a story covering these changes or relevant info pertaining to your patient. You may title it "The Top Five VA benefits answers you need to know" and phrase it as an easygoing, inside look at how the VA benefits have changed and what that could mean for anyone affected by them.

2) Google + Local LOVES Local Events

This may be one of the super-ninja secret of online marketing. I suggest you talk about local events! Creating articles about current local events and tying them back to you is a phenomenal way to create local brand awareness. As your local audience make these connections online it naturally helps your ranking as Google's algorithm is hard wired for this. I can provide an example of this. Imagine the next event in your community. Or, it could be a series of events that are regularly scheduled. Is there any controversy surround the event? Is parking a disaster? Is this good or bad for the community overall? Do you have suggestions for parking or top restaurants or activities for those attending? You may decide to write an article about this. The double benefit is, your name is out there in the community and it will undoubtedly help you with your rankings because Google's algorithms will calculate your local relevancy. This will be more impactful as you can provide keywords about your location that Google + Local specifically indexes for relevancy.

I want to suggest you resist the urge to discuss anything about your practice in the local community blogs. The point is to get your name out there for both the community and Google as mentioned above. This really is about creating top of mind awareness. It's about being you, everywhere. You have to think strategically about the long term goal. Too many people seek the short term battle win at the expense of the long war. Take the high road and avoid at all possible costs, discussing your practice. **TIP:**

You can always refer to yourself with your keywords! Don't overdo it, but it's perfectly fine to use things like "As a _____ (insert target niche / business type here) in Atlanta, GA, I'm always surprised when...". That's the best of both worlds!

Another great tip is to be proactive- go to a local newspaper site, see what they're covering and link back to the newspaper site and talk about it. It's easy research!

Always remember, people only do business and they only trust their healthcare decisions to those they like and trust. Your local community blogs are far reaching in communicating to your viewer how in touch you are with your community and its issues. Also, isn't it okay just to distribute content for the joy of it becoming regarded as entertainment and enjoyable reading? Please stop and think about that. Too many doctors, dentists and (you fill in the blank here, if needed) are too serious about their work and the mission. Yes, I understand the health profession is a serious business. Yet, there is a lighter side to it isn't there? This likeability factor goes a long way. This viewer is way more likely to remember you because of your involvement. Remember, the 60% earlier in the book that were open to it or not thinking about it. Well when they are, you are increasing the chances you will be remembered.

A good rule of thumb is to split it up half and half: focus both on health care articles and local, relevant stories. Combined with the added dimension of your team's regular contribution, can provide a three-prong to maximizing your blog impact.

Here's an interesting thought: Blogging has been around now for about fifteen to twenty years. It's honest and truly one of the top ways to generate new business and it's obviously an incredible tool for sharing information. Think about it, whether you knew it or not, Tumblr has over 100 million blogs. Most of these blogs are in some way reposted to the hundreds of social sites at some point.

Video Blogging or Vlogging for short

The new trend is vlogging.

On the whole, we are no longer just writing status updates and posting pictures. The upcoming trend is video blogging. It's been said that one of the key features of leadership is the ability to predict what's next. An interesting trend to lead and to watch is how social media is tapping into this. Many of the big players in social media are recognizing and facilitating their member's ability to video blog.

Vlogging is short for blogging with video. A blog that primarily uses video to distribute a message is called a vlog. Not many of these currently exist, but many trend watchers say that it's only a matter of time until the intimate format of video begins to replace static text and images. Faster bandwidth speeds and cheaper bandwidth make this possible.

We have Apple to thank for this as well as their other two million breakthroughs. With the release of the iPod with video in 2005, Apple developed a medium for video, opening the door for the era of the vlog. A viewer streaming video is absolutely comparable to a 1970s television viewer, but the content creation is highly distributed rather than centralized, and the viewer would have access to thousands or even millions of channels rather than just a few dozen or hundred or six in the 1970s example.

I've heard the first videoblog aired in early 2000. Yet, this medium did not truly emerge until 2004, when small communities of vloggers began to emerge. I think that we will see the trend continue with websites like Google Video and YouTube offering free storage space.

One of the key problems with vlogging is that currently, there are no unified standards for tagging metadata. Or in other words, tags that identify what the videos are about. Search engine "spiders" can't watch a blog, decide what it's about, and index it accordingly. This may be the one thing that prevents vlogging from really taking off. But as a reader of this book I'll let you in on a secret and definitely a best practice. It's the concept of multi-casting. The idea here is to take your vlog and have it transcribed! Real simple right? Yes in fact it is! I'm not suggesting you do it obviously. The transcription can be posted somewhere on the same page as the video and will absolutely help your rankings. I will discuss more about vlogging in the next chapter on social media.

THE FACTS PLEASE!

- Blogging is an important key to the success of your marketing campaign: make sure to blog at least once a week with a post that is between 250 and 800 words. If possible, blog twice a week; this is the optimal number and blogging more than twice a week won't help you more. Involve your team as much as possible. A diversified point of view and perspective will go a long way with your SEO outcomes.

- You don't need to make every blog about what you do specifically; you can and should alternate between what you do and community events.

- Be natural; this will help you be more accessible to your clients, and thus garner more page views and attention from people looking to comment on the blog as well as make you more viewable and able to be indexed by each of the major search engines.

Chapter Five

SOCIALCASTING: USING FACEBOOK, INSTAGRAM, LINKEDIN, TWITTER AND THE REST

This chapter title may have an emotional response for you. You may be charged up and ready to tackle this chapter. Or, you may be indifferent. You may react negatively to some or all of these sites. There is one certainty; your online strategy is intimately connected to how you use these resources. Maybe you don't want to believe that, but it is still a statement of fact and not likely to change.

I especially like the reaction I get when I discuss Twitter with clients. Even the name and rules about content seem kind of strange. Yet, I'm going to make a statement that I believe strongly. Twitter is probably the most useful tool of all the sites listed in bringing new patients into your world. I'll back up that statement during this chapter.

Why Social Media?

Simply put: Social media is the driving force in how all the search engines determine what relevant material is. It was common practice for many years for "black hat" type of SEO tacticians to game the system as mentioned earlier. Tactics included article spinning (articles that hardly made sense from overuse of changing of certain words), bots and irrelevant links – most of this categorized as spam. Social media, however, does the vetting ingeniously by how it's designed. Users of social media sites aren't going to share links that are spam with each other. Obviously, they are sharing real content – things that matter. Google and other search engines now have built into their algorithms how relevant content is by social sharing. If real people are posting content and that content was deemed valuable enough to share and comment on by many people, then it's pretty logical that it should be indexed. - The average time on Google is six minutes. The average time on Facebook is seven hours. Where should you be focused?

- Facebook, as of this writing, has over 1.11 billion users. To put that into perspective, that means Facebook has more users than the US population; this is very important in terms of saturation.

Instagram passed Twitter in daily activity use in 2012, according to ComScore. In fact, ComScore's data shows that Instagram's daily active user count had increased almost increased tenfold in the six-month period starting in March 2012, when it had 886,000 daily active visitors. Twitter's mobile user numbers had increased as well, but at a much slower rate. Part of this may simply be due to the fact that Instagram is a younger company, but it's impressive nonetheless.

What these statistics should show you is that social media is a very, very powerful force in today's cultural mindset, and it's only getting stronger. Social media is here to stay, and more and more people every day are participating and receiving advice from their friends and family about great stories or services that they received.

The 800 pound elephant in the room Google has taken notice of this and has answered with its own social network. In this chapter, we're going to take a look at each of the major social networks and discuss what should be your strategy for each – not in total detail, but enough to whet your appetite for what's possible?

The Social Networks

With your social media strategy, there are currently three huge players that we need to focus on: Facebook, Twitter, and LinkedIn. I trust you won't conclude that you can ignore the other important sites like YouTube, Instagram, Google+ and the several others (always changing). These will be discussed in depth. The question will always get back to resources and prioritizing those resources.

The thrust of your marketing strategy, I believe, should absolutely focus on these Big Three.

Before we dive in to each, you need to understand that each of these three is handled completely different. The formula for Twitter will not work for YouTube, LinkedIn, or any other site for that matter. What works on Facebook may work on one or several. Truly, the "art" of designing an optimally run marketing initiative is recognizing patterns. I hope the next statement does not sound self-serving. With experience, it's not hard to miss patterns. Having worked with hundreds of companies and medical practices through the years, the key to the online play is to understand how each of the social media sites rank relevancy and determine what characteristics take priority. After that, the art of maximizing return falls squarely on guessing, measuring and adjusting the tactics.

Facebook

Facebook's almost conquered the world. Estimates suggest usage at 1.1 Billion. That's billion with a B. Just smaller than China's population of 1.3 billion and about three times the population of the US (313M), Facebook is a force to be reckoned with. By the way, India is number 2 and Indonesia is number 4. I was well aware of the top three. I don't know why Indonesia surprised me, but it did.

Here are some important questions: What is your approach to Facebook? What content gets best results? Algorithmically speaking, what's most engaging? How do we measure viewer response? What content gets the best response? Why can't we reach more "fans" with our updates? What kind of content should we be sharing? What are the "first do's", "must do's" and "should do's" for

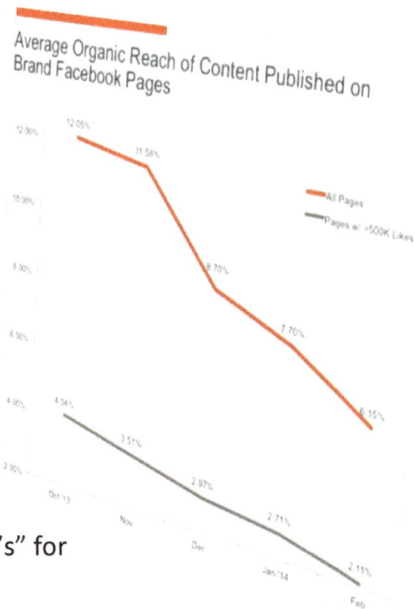

Average Organic Reach of Content Published on Brand Facebook Pages

us to tackle? I know I've asked a lot of questions. Let me provide you some hard facts from our experience. Facebook has changed. Apparently what worked before does not work now. Your strategy has to adapt. My observation is that it sucks when the rules of engagement are changed without notice. How does this happen? The curt answer is that the social media sites, particularly Facebook, had to change. Whether the reason is maturity or technological advancement or both, change was inevitable. The complete answer is that both maturity and technological advancement played a part in the change. If you think about it, the incredible volume of content required that the rules change. The sheer volume of over a billion users and over eighteen million business pages is a testament to that.

Many writers that blog on social media feel that the eventuality of organic search relevancy may hit zero. In layman's terms this means that the content you provide has a very slim chance of actually getting read. In 2012, Facebook controversially restricted its organic reach of business pages (or branded pages) to about 16%.

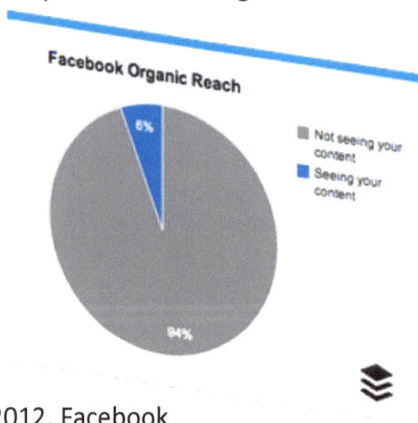

Facebook Organic Reach

- Not seeing your content
- Seeing your content

6%

94%

Expectations are this percentage will eventually reach zero. This trend is observable in this graph.

Once upon a time, content was king on Facebook. While Facebook ads used to be applauded for their micro-targeting brilliance, the ads are way more essential to businesses now. Because Facebook has changed – and continues to change – its algorithm, commercial content continues to drop in news feed ranking. The vast majority of your Facebook business audience – about 95 percent – will not see your content or posts! Clearly, as the graph illustrates, advertising is no longer just for major brands or rich law firms. If you want more of your audience to see your content, cough up the cash!

The question really is if Facebook is now a "paid channel" or are there opportunities to continue "earned conversations"? In other words, what is this segment of the social media marketing focus worth going forward? Should practitioners and their team responsible for social marketing move on from Facebook? I think moving forward; Facebook's appeal and sheet volume of users will continue its viability. The power in Facebook is that fans will still see a brand's content in their newsfeed and if the content is interesting enough, will share it. A "friends' recommendation will still carry a lot of weight with ranking content. Yet, how does Facebook calculate what gets on the newsfeed? Of course, no one but Facebook knows the full answer. Facebook itself has reported that over 100,000 individual weights comprise its model.   The few elements that apparently carry more weight are

- Affinity – the relationship with the user and how often interaction takes place
- Weight – top priority goes to video and photos, with posting
- Current – more current equals higher weight

This is a graphic courtesy of PostRocket that summarizes this.

I believe the biggest takeaway from this is just how <u>critical</u> it is to convert your social media audience and particularly your Facebook audience into one that is independent of these channels...meaning until this audience has opted in to your process such as an email campaign, etc. you may lose them. Meaning these 2.2 Billion eyeballs are Facebook's – not yours until you do.

Twitter — it is very hard to ignore a social site that boasts over 500M users. Yet this is precisely what most small and medium size practitioners do when it comes to Twitter. Some call it stupid. Some call it inconsequential. Primarily because Twitter is the most open social network out there, it should be one of your key marketing channel strategies.

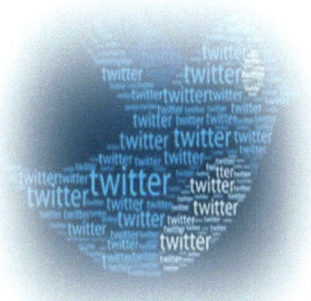

 Why do I write that? Simply put, every single tweet (a "tweet" is what each individual Twitter post is called) is indexed by Google. Other social networks, like Facebook and LinkedIn, require a username and password to see most of their content. With Twitter, there is no requirement to log in to see individual tweets. Consequently, Google can index every tweet. This has a huge bearing on Google's page rankings. Google and the other search engines use the universe of tweets to help gauge a site or a page's relevance. Pages that reference many links from Twitter are deemed higher importance.

Let me just cut to the chase and tell you exactly what you can do to make Twitter your best friend without spending a minute on it...hire someone that can. All joking aside, for my clients we preplan each month in advance. We know that an effective Twitter campaign entails anywhere from seven to ten "tweets" daily. So, these are setup in advance and then are programmed to broadcast at various predetermined times during the month. Voila! It's done! There are a number of online solutions that make this possible.

Here are some best practices we incorporate when we manage our client's Twitter accounts as part of a larger, comprehensive marketing effort. Keeping in mind the 140 character limit, I'm amazed at how many tweets seek to maximize this out. Simply stated if you keep your message to 120 characters or less, you provide your audience the ability to re-tweet your message with room for their name and a very short lead in or intro. Try to follow only those who are somehow aligned with what you do. The search engines will reward the fact that these followers are keyed in to your message and closely align their message around yours. Meaning there are similarities and there's a commonality of language.

Make certain you stay on point. Don't stray too far from the topics that are relevant to your practice. It would be wise to take the advice from earlier in the book on SEO and the intelligent use of keywords. If you appear robotic and focused on search engine content as opposed to providing good content, you are doing a disservice to your entire effort.

When the conversation comes up, most people I talk to about Twitter don't know that the site has video and picture capabilities. You can imbed a video or photo in a tweet so that your viewer doesn't need to navigate away to view it. Finally, and this actually covers every social site we discuss, is to setup Google Alerts. This tool provides a way to keep track of what is being said about you and your practice. I will have more to say about this in an upcoming chapter on reputation management.

LinkedIn

LinkedIn is usually always initially ignored with the medical practitioners I work with. The usual response is that you mistakenly believe you are singularly categorized as business to consumer (B2C). Plain and simple this is flawed thinking. Why do I say that? If you look at the demographic I share in the graph on the following page I hope you recognize that these are your "best buyers". Take a minute to understand and then I will discuss this ideal patient concept in detail.

More Affluent

This site attracts a more affluent audience.

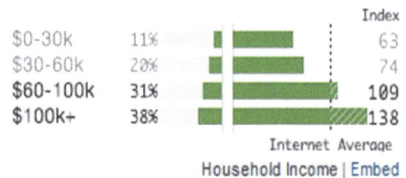

Household Income		Index
$0-30k	11%	63
$30-60k	20%	74
$60-100k	31%	109
$100k+	38%	138

Internet Average
Household Income | Embed

Graduates And Post Graduates

There is a high index of Graduates and Post Graduates here.

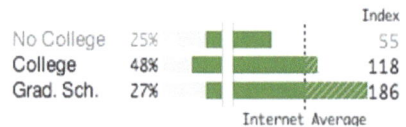

		Index
No College	25%	55
College	48%	118
Grad. Sch.	27%	186

Internet Average

Does this demographic not need what you practice? Silly question right? Of course they do! The lesson, and if I were sitting across from you my words would be emphatic, deliberate and slow, is that maybe, just maybe these are your best buyers. It's a revolutionary concept for some practitioners. One of the joys of my work is to catch the expression of my client in a eureka moment as we discuss this strategy. I ask them to pull a report with stats on what their patient spend - meaning the average transaction value. Frankly, it surprises me how few have this readily available. I'm patient enough to wait for the practice manager to get the information. On a side note this is one of the daily flash report data bit that I recommend you understand. Lo and behold when we analyze the percentage of revenue that is generated by each patient, the answer usually always is a surprise for some. The average is that 30% of the client base produces 70% of the revenue. Many times in some practices, particularly the more elective, like plastic surgery, the numbers can get to 80:20 and once in a while 90:10. Our very next exercise is to produce an "avatar" of this person. Who are they? Where do they live? Where do they socialize? How can we reach them? Do we have an automated and passive referral process in place to leverage new relationships? Candidly, we've doubled the revenues of many practices just focusing on a dedicated campaign like this. In every case, Linkedin has been a big part of the initiative.

GOOGLE+:

What makes Google+ different from Facebook, Linkedin, Youtube and Twitter?

This is not Google's 1st attempt at social. There are many social networks, but let's focus on the big 4 Facebook, Linkedin, Youtube and Twitter. Understanding how these sites operate helps explain Google+

Youtube – I make a video. You search for it and can watch, share, or comment on my video. As a search based network this is the most open network of them all. Few people use the subscribe function as a social element.

Linkedin – Use to be: Here is my resume please hire me — Now is: I need a job, I collaborate with my colleagues & vendors to learn and grown in groups, and I get / answer questions. The most closed network of the 4, you must know my email, already have worked with me, or be in a group with me to connect.

Twitter – I can push information out to many people and this information can be spread quickly. Google indexes this network, which is a bonus. As many people as are on Twitter can follow my updates. You can follow me and I do not need to follow you. Information is sent out in short bursts and interaction takes place both on Twitter (in a short conversation style) and off Twitter (follow this link to see this video, read my blog, etc.)

Facebook - The current king of social media. Facebook is about "friendships". You and I must mutually like each other to share information. I can post information with hopes that this information is seen on your News Feed. There is no guarantee my information will be seen by my friends. Facebook controls information and uses an algorithm called Edge to determine what information they believe I want to see. There is a great business component with Pages.

Google+ What makes you

so different?

From a big picture Google+ is all about connecting all of your computer uses both online and offline in one place. This includes your documents,

spreadsheets, applications, videos, everything being available in one location and everything being one click from something you can share.

This brings us to the MAJOR DIFFERENCE of Google+

So this is great, I can share all my information from my site to my expense report, but I don't want to share everything with the world. My uncle does not need to know about everything about my work and I need to protect some elements of my personal life from my clients.

Google+ plus has created a revolutionary function called CIRCLES. Circles control both the stream of information out and in. People you connect with are organized into different circles.

How do Circles work and why are they important?

GOOGLE+
CIRCLES

1) You can create any circle you want. Examples of my circles include: Following, Friends, Best Friends, Employees, Clients, Vendors, Very Smart Marketing People, Fellow coaches and business growth planners, Funny Peeps, Family

2) The people you connect with can be in multiple circles. Some people that are Very Smart Marketing People are also my Friends

3) I can choose to send information to one, or more, circles. This information will appear on their wall or can be sent as a message. The great thing is if I share something with my client circle only then no one else sees that post on their feed. Maybe we just got back from a family vacation and I want to share the photos with my family and friends but do not want to bother my vendors, clients, and the general public with the images.

4) I can choose to see information from one or more circles in my feed. Instead of being told what content an algorithm thinks I would like to see, I can choose my content feed based on my circles. This allows me to quickly and easily navigate from one set of feeds to the next. Since you can have people in multiple circles, I know that I am seeing what I want from whom I want.

Here are a few other features to Google+

- Multiple Video Chat. Google+ will allow you to connect with up to 10 people on live video chat at the same time. The feature is smooth and audio is good. A real great way to connect with people for virtual meetings. The best part of this feature is the person talking gets the main screen.

- Larger image and video display on the wall. When you post a video or images they are about 3 times larger on the wall when compared to Facebook.

- Easy navigation to all of Google's functions. While on Google+ you can search the web, see your gmail messages, and access your Google Documents.

- Simple share option. Very similar to Facebook, Google uses both a +1 button (similar to Facebook's like) and a "share this post" option.

- 1 click and you can add someone. If you see a name in a post, find someone in your friends feed, or stumble upon someone of interest you can add them without navigating to their page. This is very convenient. When you hover over their name you a box appears giving you the option to add them to a circle.

Setting up Google+ is simple. Similar to other social media outlets, there is an area for information about you, pictures, website URLs, and basic data. As always, only share what you are comfortable sharing. Make sure your about me section has benefits to working with you and keywords for your industry. Like Linkedin there is a title are that you should also include keywords about your area of practice.

Press Releases

Certainly critical, press releases need to be an integral part of both your online and offline marketing efforts. Besides keeping you

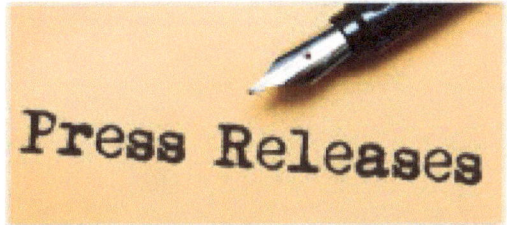

relevant, your press releases serve an important function in your SEO work. It is a viable and effective way to drive traffic to your site. The secret to writing effective releases is to first understand what your outcome is. Is it to create brand awareness? Are you looking to increase attendance at an upcoming community event? Are you releasing news just stay relevant? These are the usual big three but there are a multiple reasons to stay consistent in releasing stories.

Usually the first question I get asked is how do I write a great press release? As you would expect your press releases need to be relevant to the audience. It should announce something new and exciting in your business that your reader will find interesting. Announcing the last certification you successfully completed, as an example, is probably not something anyone else would find interesting...unless they were in your field. Discussing a new breakthrough that translates into a benefit for your reader is something they would probably be more interested in.

Your press release should follow a format. Let's discuss each section of your press release and I'll add some best practices for each, both SEO and for keeping the reader's attention.

Your Headline. The headline needs to immediately capture your reader's attention. The headline needs to grab them quickly. It's critical that your headline be in the active tense. For example, instead of "doctor group opened new practice location close to the new mall", you should write doctor group opens new..." It's not important if the event is in the past or the future. The heading is the only place in the release where you use the present tense. The rest of the release should use the correct tense. If the group already opened the location, then the rest of the story should state it correctly. The first paragraph is the who, what, when, where and why. It should be brief, maybe three to four sentences long. Understand that the first reader is the media screener and he or she may not get past the first paragraph, so make it good. Write the release as if you were a journalist. The story should flow like any other news announcement. Avoid becoming "salesy" with words like "something not to be missed" or other promotional jargon. The length of your story should stay between 400 and 600 words. This is critical for SEO and for not overdoing it on your reader. If the search engines can't index your story because the message is too long or gets diluted, you probably won't get much traction search-wise.

The links you see on web sites connecting a word or phrase to a related page are called "anchor text," This is a great way to guide your reader to additional information (eliminating the need to write an excessively long press release), anchor text – when used properly – can also deliver significant SEO benefits back to your site. Do not over-link. At most two links in your story should suffice. Use your most important keyword in your headline. Remember the rule, less is more. A clear, concise message resonates well with your readers. It's also critical for your other reader...the search engine. Too many keywords can sound robotic and manipulative. It will also dilute the message.

There are several other factors worth mentioning. A title tag is at the top of each website page. The title tag hugely influences how well your story is optimized. Your header and sub header both help determine how your Search Engine Results Page description reads. Because headlines and sub headlines are designed to grab your readers' attention, you better make it good.

With most press release services you can submit your press release for free or via paid inclusion. Paying for inclusion gives you the benefit of faster indexing into the search engine news services and natural search engine result pages. Google usually picks up the news a few hours after release. It then takes a few days to show up in normal organic searches.

Just the Facts:

- Social media is one of the most important forces in marketing today: you can't ignore it. You need a plan to maximize the impact you have with each of the social sites. Social sites are always evolving. It's critical to anticipate "what's next".

- The three biggest social media players right now are Facebook, Twitter, and LinkedIn: you need to systemize a process for setting up blog updates to each social network

- Google+, though new, is rapidly growing: make sure you incorporate your strategy with this.

- Press releases are an extremely important part of your online marketing strategy, so much so that you should have your marketing business do it for you and cut down on the immense amount of time you're spending on it.

- Social media is rapidly changing, and no single strategy will stay effective forever; make sure to keep updated to stay ahead of the game!

CHAPTER SIX
HOW TO USE ONLINE DIRECTORIES TO GET MORE PATIENTS

Directory listings have been around since the inception of the online

world. Directory listings are, in short, the online version of the Yellow

Pages: Super Pages, YellowPages.com, Yahoo Local, Bing Places, Google

Places / Google + Local, etc.

These

directories are

commonly called "citations". There are literally thousands of them

competing for eyeballs. Thankfully there are only about 15 major ones

where you want to be listed. The majority of these services allow for a free listing. You should not need anything more than that. However, a paid listing or preferred listing may be right for you depending on your market, but do everything else first and after you have a baseline for your online success, test the gain in calls or emails you receive by opting for a paid enhancement to a directory listing. In this way you can measure the real cost/benefit of the investment. Some directories, like InfoUSA, are even more important and you must be sure your information is correct because other directories pull information from these.

These directories have gained importance when Google moved its local search returns to its main page, using Google Places / Google + Local. The algorithm that determines which Google Places / Google + Local business listings belong on the first page of Google search results takes a great deal of its weighting consideration by searching to see if your business is listed elsewhere. If you're in 5, 10, or even 15 directory listings (with reviews in the local area) that's going to look very good in Google's ranking system. We'll get to reviews in the next chapter, but suffice it to say that directory listings with reviews are very helpful; if your competition is getting more reviews than you, they probably will enjoy first page rankings while you won't.

You're going to want to be on multiple directories; there are some services out there that will do this for you, but quite often the best way to do it is to do it manually. You really want to be in control of this— some services are pretty spotty, and they'll slip in shady techniques or insist that you stay out of the process. It's not that hard or time-consuming, and we recommend doing it manually; just go through the top 10-15 directory listings, Enter everything asked for. Make sure to use keywords and geo-location in your description; geolocation is just an SEO term for city / state.

How to List Yourself

It's a pretty easy process to list yourselves, all things considered. You just have to go to these directories and their websites, and list yourself. Some are paid, but many are free and just try to upcharge you with different services once you've listed yourself on the directories. Paid directories are really not necessary. Our experience is that, done correctly, you never need to pay for directory listings or any of the extra services the free ones offer you. The skillful use of keywords and geolocation will do wonders toward first page ranking. . We've had many, many clients top-ranked in Google Places / Google + Local who never paid for directory listings, and it's most likely the case that you'll never have to pay for a directory listing or upcharge either. That is not to say that these additional paid services won't provide more traffic and clients to your business, but don't start there.

WARNING:

Big warning here! This is a problem that we run into with many practitioners that office together. . The problem occurs if each of them goes in and creates their own listing. This results in multiple listings for each and one for the office as a whole. When Google queries the directory listings, it gets confused at the multiple entries for the one address; it thinks it's an attempt to game the system and may ignore them all.

You want to go in and be very, very careful that you only have one listing; search for your address, business name, other people in the office, anything you can think of to identify multiple listings. If you do have multiple listings and didn't know it, delete them all! Get down to zero and start from scratch; it's much better that way. If for whatever reason you can't delete them all, at least get down to one and edit that one as best you can.

Another important thing to remember when you're doing directory listings is to make sure to use keywords and geolocation only in the short / long descriptions that the directory listings give you. Do not use keywords in your business name! This is why you have a keyword-rich URL; if the URL was the business name you'd have to use that and not get the keyword benefit. Google does not like to see business names stuffed with keywords and geo-location; that will definitely hurt you in the long run.

This can be turned to your advantage, depending on how dedicated you are to this strategy; some of our sharper clients have actually changed their business name to include keywords and geolocation, like Radiology Group of Orlando.

If the directory listing has suggested keywords, consider using them; it probably looks very similar to the Yellow Pages categories you are used to seeing. Some places give you a chance to type in yours, in which case do so. Don't go crazy, however, because Google only values about 3-4 keywords; anything after that they consider gaming the system and just ignore.

Here is a list of directories that your business needs to be listed on.

1. Google Places / Google + Local

2. Yahoo!

3. YellowBot

4. Yelp

5. WhitePages

6. MapQuest

7. SuperPages

8. CitySearch

9. YellowBook

10. Local.com

11. MerchantCircle

There are about 40 more directory listings that we list our clients on. Some of these directory listings are more relevant today then they will be a year from now. Do the research and find at least 15 more directories to list your business on top of the core 11 above.

Google Places / Google + Local

Google Places / Google + Local, though technically a listing, is probably the most important "final step" with your listing. Get the rest of the directory listings in first, wait a month or so until you have a few reviews, and then create your Google Places / Google + Local page. This wait time is very important- it's so important, in fact, that we begin an engagement with clients who already have a Google Places / Google + Local listing before this structure is in place we sometimes advise them to delete it and start over unless it's already in the top 7 listings. If it's not on the first page, delete it, do this process, and add it a month later.

The reason behind this is that when you create a Google Places / Google + Local page, it looks for all the information about you: Directory listings, blogs, reviews, etc. If you've done all the things we've talked about it should help rocket way up to the top of the list once you create it; if you want to be on the first page, waiting those four weeks to make a Google Places / Google + Local listing makes a huge, huge difference in your ranking!

Also, another powerful, yet rarely discussed advertising medium is Pay per Click advertising...the best example of which is Google AdWords.

AdWords is pound-for-pound the single quickest way to get your business listed on Page #1 of Google. You can do it in 10 minutes or less. It will cost you a few dollars a day (when you know what you are doing). Or it could cost you thousands (if you don't). The key is to have your ads show ONLY in your geographical area. Our recommendation is to find someone who is skilled at AdWords and pay them to do your ads. It will pay off for you in the end.

Just The Facts:

- There are hundreds of directory listings out there; be smart and only join the 10-15 that are the biggest and most relevant (yelp, AVVO, etc.)

- You can pay people to put you on directories, but the best and cheapest way is to do it yourself. Most directories are free. They'll try to get you with up-sells and add-ons, but don't bother. They don't help.

- Don't put keywords in your business name in the directories; Google doesn't like it unless those keywords are part of your business name.

- You'll be tempted to put up a Google Places / Google + Local along with the directories, but don't. It's best to wait a month or so and create after you've gotten a few reviews.

Chapter Seven
IN WITH THE NEW: HOW TO USE ONLINE REVIEWS TO DRIVE YOUR MARKETING

It's not well known that Google relies heavily on reviews created by customers in order to rank a site. The logic is that if a local business is reviewed, then someone's been there. The review comments give an indication of the quality of the location and whether or not it deserves to be ranked higher or lower. Many of these reviews allow reviewers to give star ratings, which are even more influential: Google scrapes these numbers automatically to do a sort of website litmus test, a judgment of whether or not the establishment is overall positive or negative.

In fact, Google has recently adjusted the Google Places / Google + Local page user interface to prominently display the "Write a review" button to specifically encourage reviews within Google's own systems.

Review sites are, in general, the directory listings we talked about earlier; Google uses the info to determine how your customers interact with you – whether or not you are important in your local marketplace.

Another key point to this strategy is that many of your competitors are simply not getting reviews at all.

You may notice many of your key competitors have no reviews, or a low number of them! As a result, you don't need to get hundreds of reviews on your directory listings and Google Places / Google + Local page; you just need to have a little consistency and make sure you're getting a couple reviews a month on just 2 or 3 different directories (one of which must be Google Places / Google + Local).

To start, you're going to need to size up how many reviews you need to rank. Do some review research on your keywords; type them into Google and see how many reviews the top ranked results have. If they have five reviews, you need ten- if they have thirty; you've got some work to do. Keep in mind that these are total reviews: for example, if you need twenty reviews, you can spread it over four months. That's just five reviews per month, which is certainly doable, and we'll talk about how to get those reviews shortly.

Review Sites

Which review sites should you focus on? How do you figure out which ones are worth your time and which ones aren't?

Thankfully, there's a fairly efficient way to do it. First off, half the work is done: many of these review sites are also directory listings, and you've already listed yourself on the top directory listings. What you have to do, then, is to do a Google keyword search in your location and go through the pages at the bottom.

For the most part, you're just interested in the top 5 directories that are already listed; make a list of your directory listings and cross-reference which ones appear first in the Google keyword search. For example, if you are a dentist is Dallas, you should search Dallas and then your business name. Then look at the results and find the first 3-5 listings that refer to an online directory site like Yelp, CitySearch, or Super Pages. The 3-5 that appears first are the ones you're going to want to focus on.

It's also OK if you don't find 5; you may only find 2 or 3 at the beginning, and that's fine. This is normal- sometimes it can take search engines quite some time to properly index all the information out there. To give you some perspective, there are about ten thousand new websites created every day; this is a gigantic amount for search engines to index, and so often there's a lag time as the search engines crawl the pages and index them. Your mission here is to find the ones that are ranked, and of those find the top ranked ones; these are the ones where you're going to focus your review techniques!

TIP:

If there are a great number of reviews for your keyword niche, consider focusing on one or two. Ordinarily, a _____(insert target niche /) don't generally have to deal with this, since the _____market isn't normally saturated with reviews. If you have a competitor that's saturated with reviews, however, Google their keywords and see which review sites are consistently being pulled up the most; focus all your review efforts on those. As an example, if your keyword is "_____" and the majority of reviews are being pulled from CitySearch, then CitySearch is the best place to start.

Getting Reviews

Now that we've narrowed down our target directories, let's get reviews on them. We'll start with your current clients: it'll be easier to get reviews from them, as they're right in the middle of working with you.

It's important to note here that we understand that _____s are, depending on the state, sometimes not allowed to ask for testimonials. You need to understand this because this is important: you are not asking for a testimonial. We are very clear on this point: you are simply asking for someone to go to a website and put in a review. It's on a public forum where they could leave the review with or without your assistance. You're going to want to have a card produced, see our sample below, that you hand to your clients as they walk out the door; this card will tell them where to go and how to write a review. This is absolutely crucial!

WARNING:

You cannot, under any circumstances, go in to these websites and create the reviews for your clients. They also can't give you the reviews and you write the reviews; Google will know from the IP address that these reviews are all coming from the same location and they will ignore it at best and hurt your ranking or get rid of your listing altogether at the worst. This is true even if they are real reviews that clients mailed you; a common scammer trick is to have teams of people writing multiple reviews, and as such Google is searching that spam out and penalizing that harshly. Under no circumstances should your clients write reviews from your location; they need to write the review there. This is vital! This also extends to other computers in your office. There is a common setup we see fairly often; businesses will have a "review" computer set up in the office, where clients can go and enter in a review. This falls into the same trap as the scenario above, and we always warn clients against this when we see it: Google is tracking these reviews, and even though it's not you typing, unfortunately, it's coming from the same place. Google can't distinguish these from scammers who employ that same trick, and thus having this "review station" isn't going to help you at all. They absolutely, positively have to do it on their computer in their home or business; there's no way around this and it's very important for you to remember this!

2nd WARNING:

Be very careful about who you hire to do your review process! There are many companies out there that will over promise on providing a lot of reviews, yet aren't able to deliver on that promise. Many times, these services are near-spam type businesses that just create all the reviews themselves and post them from one IP address. Not only is this not going to help you, this sort of review fabrication is against the law. If you absolutely must, make sure you build your process with a proven agency / partner. We provide our clients with an entire review process whitepaper.

The best way to get these reviews, as mentioned above, is to hand out your card. Don't stop there, however: another great way is mailing or emailing clients asking for reviews (see our sample below). Make it a team effort- insert into the email where you're ranking and where your competitors are ranking, and explain that you want to get to the top and get reviews as well.

Remember, you should not be focusing strictly on Google Places / Google + Local. You want to send people to a few different directories. You do of course want reviews going to Google Places / Google + Local as well, but you need to diversify. Provide your patients cards with other review sites on them as well, such as Yelp, CitySearch, and the others that you've identified in your target directory listings. Try not to put them all on one card, however: it looks cramped, awkward, and unprofessional. A card per review site looks much better, and it'll work better in getting clients to go to the review sites for you.

 The same goes for your emails; your clients may already have an account on one of these review sites and then it would be even easier for them to leave a review saying what a wonderful job you did! This also helps even more since identified reviews count even more than anonymous ones!

Again, it's important to note that these are not testimonials: these are things your patients can do on their own. In fact, you're simply trying to encourage a behavior that's already happening: don't be surprised if, when you start this process, you already have a couple of reviews online. All you're doing is encouraging this process: you're saying "Hey, there are these review sites out there and having reviews help us. You might do it already, and if you liked our service, your review will really help us!" You'll find, more often than not, that people are more than willing to help you out in this regard. They'll visit these sites and fill out reviews, and this is super-important: it's one of the driving forces behind the Google Places / Google + Local rankings, and by having this steady system of reviews you're ensuring your higher ranking!

Just the Facts:

- Reviews are very important, and should not be overlooked: search the review sites and find out which ones you should be focusing on.

- Make sure you have a system in place to get users to review you: this is different from testimonials!

- Whatever you do, don't have a computer in your office for clients to write reviews (and absolutely don't write their reviews for them). Google requires the reviews to be written by the client on a computer outside of the office, and so the reviews need to be done on the client's own computer!

- Be careful about who you hire to do your review marketing: some marketers will promise huge numbers but write fake reviews with duplicate content and severely damage your Google ranking!

CHAPTER EIGHT
AUTOMATING YOUR PROCESS

Follow-up strategies are a vital segment of any Internet marketing strategy, and it's equally vital that you automate it as much as possible; many businesses will attempt to do this manually, but the overhead required to manually implement isn't feasible for most businesses. It's vital that you don't spend manual time fielding emails and responding one by one; we've had clients in the past that literally sent out e-mail newsletters every week by hand. If somebody new came in, they'd get manually added to this email list.

That sort of system may work in the beginning, but it's easy to see that it doesn't scale up well at all; you need an automated method of follow-up that both preserves quality but also scales out well, freeing up resources and keeping your Internet marketing strategy running smoothly and efficiently!

Follow-up Framework

Initially, we have to talk about the framework for follow-up: when we're talking about follow-up, we're talking about traffic generated to you. We're not talking about people that come in through the door necessarily. We're talking about follow-up that happens when the person finds you; you need a follow-up strategy whether or not the contact is initiated by phone, email, or online via the website.

When a new client gets to your website and opts in with their name, phone number, and email address, they go into your funnel. Your funnel is the resource you have where you capture your leads and market to them specifically from there. The reason for this is that they've invested in you by providing you this information—they're a "warm lead" and obviously interested, and you have to get to them fast! The whole function of the funnel is to provide you with a resource that enables this sort of rapid response to whatever communication the client happened to initiate.

The best way to do this is to set up a basic auto-responder system. This system will provide two things to you: it's going to alert you that someone's given you information, and it's going to send them a message immediately. There are a couple of ways to do this, and later on we'll talk about different techniques including texting and direct voicemail. The most traditional and common auto-responder, however, is an email. Your potential clients should be getting this immediately after they submit their information on your web page. There are many services that provide this type of auto-responder systems: Constant Contact, AWeber, Infusionsoft, Office AutoPilot, etc. Whichever service you use, make sure they have a system in place capable of capturing names, storing names in an organized way, and making it as easy and automated as possible to send out those auto-responders.

You also need to have a strategy in place for phone numbers. If someone gives you their phone number, you should not only email them right away, but also email someone in your office right away a note that says "Hey, this person called interested in this. Here's their number." The reason for this is that the Internet is 24 hours; it doesn't close, it's always open, and your website is happily receiving visitors all around the clock. Your office hours, however, are only during the day; if your office hours are nine to four, for example, you won't be answering phones at ten in the evening.

The reason for emailing your office member is that if somebody comes in at night and submits their information, they get an immediate email; when your team gets in the next morning at nine, they can see the email and know someone tried to get in touch. They can then pick up the phone and say "Hi, this is _____ from

_____. I saw you downloaded our special report- I hope it helped you out. I'm just calling to ask if there's anything we can help you with." This is a very personal follow-up to a warm lead, with an emphasis on the personal. We can't stress that enough—you're a local business providing a service to the community and you need to reach out and make those personal connections. The bigger the step, the better; an automated email is the minimum bar to entry. If they've gone through the trouble of giving you their email, you need to say thanks, email back, and throw in a special report; maybe email them again a few days later with another message. These should be automated; you can have a few templates for these emails that you can send out to your warm leads.

It's very important to implement this email / phone call system and use it regularly. This isn't e-commerce, and we're not going to close any deals online; there's no shopping cart, no impulse buy button that's going to magically give you clients without any legwork. You are still a local business, and we're engaged in local Internet marketing- you can't just send out email and expect things to happen. You need to get that phone call or office visit to seal the deal!

Another good best practice is to email out one of your blog posts per month. Just take one of your blog posts per month, any one of them, and fire it out to everyone on your email lists. It's very easy to send out what's called a "broadcast message" to anyone on your email list still marked as open to receiving communication from you. This may be more of a long term strategy. As we discussed in chapter one, many of your potential new patients may not be "buying now". They may be open to it or not thinking about it. When you have processes and educational pieces focused on preventative strategies, you open them up to working with you. These periodic emails will let them remember who you are.

Just The Facts:

- Follow-up is important, but it's equally important that your follow-up process be automated: You should not be sending out newsletters or follow-ups by hand, or adding anyone manually to lists.

- Don't just follow-up with your leads when they fill out a form: follow-up in the office as well. This lets an employee call the lead as soon as possible, while they're still warm, and shows the lead that you're friendly and ready to do business. It's important to keep regular contact with your clients: fire off a blog post at least once weekly. Ideally, twice a week with automated reposts sent to all the various social sites. Any questions about this? Again, this is a regular part of the regimen of "done for you" services. These are best practices we know work to propel any practice to top rankings on each of the search engine sites.

CHAPTER NINE
THE BOTTOM LINE: ROI AND HOW TO BE SURE YOU MAKE MORE THAN YOU SPEND

It's a fact that most traditional marketing spend will be wasted dollars.

Estimates are that 20% of your budget will produce 80% of your results.

If only you knew in advance which 20%! Experience suggests that most

marketing budgets include yellow pages with TV and radio. Most of our

clients, before they retained us, spent very little on their online

marketing, and if they are, it's an extension of the Yellow Pages that's

usually not well-tracked and often very ineffective.

Advertising online, however, has a huge advantage over traditional

advertising methods normally used by most businesses: it's

extraordinarily easy to track what's going on throughout the entire

online process. You can track pretty well what's happening in each

stage. Who has emailed, what's in the funnel, etc. This is very difficult

to do with regular advertising; quite often, the only method of

communication that traditional advertising media gives a client is a phone number. Unless you're asking them where they heard about you or you're creating a unique phone number for each ad (which is, by the way, a best practice; more on that later), you're not getting very good information at all about how your advertising budget is helping you!

In contrast to these traditional advertising methods, you can glean vast amounts of data online. You can track how many people visit, and what keywords they typed in that led them to clicking your site. If they visit your Google Places / Google + Local page, you can have instant knowledge there, including who visited, when, and how. Some directory listings have tracking data in place as well, Google Analytics included.

Google Analytics is an absolute must-have for your site. If it's not already there, ask your web designer to integrate Google Analytics with your site.

It's an absolutely essential tool for monitoring your ROI and your website, and it needs to be there.

We understand you probably have not studied online marketing in depth. It's our experience that just about every one of our clients doesn't have the time to do this on a consistent basis. That's why they hire us. They hire us to implement a system where we track all traffic on their website...and all of the calls to the office. Then at the end of the month, they get a detailed report on all activity.

We mentioned above having different phone numbers for each ad; even that is more easily tracked online. There are services online that allow you to create different unique forwarding numbers that all forward to your actual number; the only difference is that the call statistics are online and you can easily see at a glance how many calls each number received. These numbers are only forwarding numbers so no need to change your main number.

Another great tool is Google Webmaster Tools, specifically because it tells you how many people are linking to you across each of your channels and thus how well your strategy is doing overall. This should be complemented by statistics on your email funnel and auto responders—you should be able to see how many people are getting / opening your emails and keep track of that as well. On top of all that, there's your own internal CRM (Customer Relationship Management system): including your pricing structure, how many hours you and your staff are working, average time spent with each patient.

As we'll see, that's an incredibly key resource in determining your ROI. We're assuming that you already have an internal CRM in place—it is crucial for this process and many others. Discussing the process and tools to manage internal CRM is beyond the scope of this book, and there are many resources available to provide you help and support with implementing your own CRM; it's a vital step in the chain, and you need to have one before you can accurately calculate your ROI.

There are an almost unlimited number of things you can track online in order to measure your ROI, and if you're going to take anything away from this section it is this: it's imperative that you have a strong, stable, well-defined system in place in order to correctly track your ROI. Most of the clients we work with believe they have a process in place, but when it's subjected to an audit it turns out that it breaks down. It's great if you even have a system in place— it's good sense and a standard marketing practice. You're spending money, and you should want to know where that investment is going and how that investment is helping you. For an Internet marketing strategy, however, you need to go above and beyond: you need to track a comprehensive set of performance indicators and result indicators. An example monthly run down might look the following. In total, 155 people visited our site this month. Of those visits, 35 came from Google Places / Google+ Local, 120 from Google organic search, and 12 from Facebook fan pages. Of these 155 visits, we followed up with all of them; of the clients we followed up with, we closed 45, and each one of them was worth $1,200 on average.

This is very basic, and the numbers are only examples, but it will give you an idea of how you should be looking at and tracking your strategy. This allows you to really get an accurate sense of valuation from clients that find you online: Are they worth the same amount as clients who found you driving by, or from referral? We want to make sure you're capturing ROI information from those clients online, and these are extremely important statistics for you to know. Very often, we end up having to build new systems and processes for clients to get this reporting accurate; make absolutely sure that when planning out your overall Internet marketing strategy, you decide what metrics you're going to use and just how you're going to track them. We can't stress this point enough: it's vital that you have an ongoing comprehensive understanding of your critical numbers. You need to be able to measure, down to the dollar, exactly what you are spending and the return on that investment.   A minimum benchmark you should strive for is a 3:1 return on investment.

TIP: If you currently have a provider, you should request they provide you with these ROI reports. If they are unable to produce this, then you should consider replacing them.

Just The Facts:

- ROI tracking on print and TV ads is hard to track and ineffective. Online ROI tracking offers a wealth of information, and enables precise tracking on where your money is going and your return on investment.

- It's imperative that you have a strong, stable, well-defined system in place in order to correctly track your ROI. Know where your money is going, know what sites are giving you hits, and know what percentage of leads you're converting, from which sites, and how much you're converting them for on average at the very least!

- If you work with a marketing agency, it's vital that they give you these ROI reports: they can give them, and if they can't or don't want to, something is seriously wrong.

Chapter Ten
WHERE DO I GO FROM HERE?

At this point you've got a real solid foundation for pulling clients in from the web; you are ranked high and your site provides various calls to action for your potential and existing patients to follow. You're social sites are providing a consistent and predictable flow of leads and you have in place a sophisticated system of follow-up and ROI tracking that will enable you to pinpoint your highest-profit channels with incredible accuracy.

Be very careful to avoid complacency. What is working now most certainly will change soon. With that in mind, this chapter is dedicated to the trends to pay attention to.

Mobile

We've held this particular topic to the very end, but this is perhaps the most immediate of all the coming challenges for online marketing. Mobile devices are rapidly becoming the primary way of checking in online. In fact, mobile is already a driving force behind many of the search engine changes we've seen. Google is setting up its local places infrastructure because information is going mobile. Mobile search is quite different than traditional search; it's more often an immediate need. Users who search mobile are typically driven by an "I need something right now that's near me" mentality, as opposed to a more research-oriented desktop user who's more willing to sift through answers and Wikipedia articles. Very few people will be doing that on a mobile phone; most likely they're looking for a business nearby they can walk or drive to quickly.

This is great news, even for most medical and dental practices. Very often, people are out at lunch, driving around, or talking about stuff and think of their problem. More and more, they'll just think to themselves "Oh! I'll just use my phone really quick and search for an answer". The same applies to sitting around eating dinner or watching TV; chances are they have their iPhone, Android phone, or tablet sitting right next to them. Instead of waiting and looking up the answer to their problem later, they'll just pick up their mobile device and look up the answer right then and there.

If your site's not mobile-responsive or your Google Places / Google + Local page is non-existent (Google Places / Google + Local is extremely mobile friendly) chances are good you may start losing business to those who are leveraging the trend.

The mobile realm also tightens up the ranking requirements quite a bit. On a regular desktop, you've got to be in the top 7 ranking; it'd be nice to be in the top 3 or 4, but 7's the bare minimum. On mobile devices, if you're not top 2 you're not being seen; very few people scroll down on mobile phones, and often they simply tap the first or second result they see. This is important to you because mobile phones offer an unparalleled ease of use; for example, many phones like iPhone and Android offer built-in calling from the web. Users can simply tap a finger on your phone number and the smartphone dials the number automatically, without any need to ever pick up another phone. As mobile devices are more and more common, it's of critical importance that your site is mobile-friendly and sits in that A or B listing on Google's result returns!

Social

We've obviously covered a great deal of social media previously. What we didn't cover, however, is the future of social networks- how they're going to change and how that's going to impact your overall online marketing strategy.

The first and most important aspect of future social is this: eventually, social media services are going to be more than just places where people connect. In the future, social media networks are going to transform into something more search engine oriented; people will go to Facebook not just to interact, but to search for things as well. This makes it crucial that you establish your presence early on. It is not too late, and you are not behind the curve: If you're lagging, make today the day you focus on building your presence with sites like LinkedIn, Twitter, Facebook, YouTube, StumbleUpon, Digg, and other social media sites. This doesn't mean you have to interact with each of these social media networks every day or even frequently, though you're going to want to keep more in touch with the big ones as per the social network chapter. What you do want, however, is a presence; just make sure that your listings are in fact on these websites- you'll be very glad you did later.

Social networks are also getting very location-oriented as time goes on, so we can expect that trend to continue. This will eventually lead to a sort of social-mobile combo: users who are google searching while also in their Facebook mobile app. This is already a user pattern that exists, and we've noticed a rise in this user behavior in the past few years.   Users are in the Facebook app and just go to the places listing and see what's around them. The first reaction is that this makes the most sense for restaurants and bars, and these establishments are leveraging that. Yet, this is useful for businesses as well: users will note "oh, this is where so-and-so office is" and they'll remember it. You need to have this local presence, because if you're not there and you're not found, someone else will be!

This social / search hybrid that we're seeing slowly creep up will also form another important piece of Internet marketing going forward: a combination of social word-of-mouth and Google ranking. Instead of letting Google figure out who's first, more people are going to go on

Facebook and see what their friends think. Your interaction level, reviews, and presence on Facebook are going to be crucial at this stage of the game: more people are going to search there the way they're currently searching on Google. Some Internet results will still trickle through, but for the most part the results will come from the client's social networks.

This is important because people in general will gauge how their friends and family have viewed businesses very seriously: from a marketing perspective, it's a long-known and oft-proven fact that people give far more weight to opinions from friends and family than from any other source of marketing. As a result, this combo of social is search is going to be very influential, and you should keep an eye on it and stay on top of it as it progresses.

Direct Mailing to Online Source

You may wonder why we're putting direct mailing in the "What's next" category; in Internet marketing terms, direct mailing is certainly not a new trend. The reason it's here is that certain trends reestablish themselves as viable. Direct mail is making a comeback. The reason for this is partly because of its scarcity. Receiving mail every now and then, done properly, is a great idea. The suggestion is not to rely on it heavily, yet it's definitely something to keep in your marketing mix and use where appropriate.

If you are currently using direct mail and want to keep doing it, you need to find a way to incorporate Google Places / Google + Local, Facebook, your website, or a call to action in your direct mailers; you have to shift the goal to getting people online. Direct mailing with mobile is an especially attractive option. Being able to snap a picture and go straight to a website to see info or reviews or being able to text a certain number to get a special report are smart ideas to bring new patients into your world.

Texting

As mentioned with direct mailing, you can now have people text a number to receive information; they're actually entering your marketing funnel the moment they text that number. This is all automatic, too; you can have the same auto-responder system set up so that it sends texts in the same way that it sends emails. If a user puts in their mobile phone number, they get a text that says something like "We've received your name and email. Thank you very much for getting in contact! Check your email for a special report, free of charge. One of our representatives will be in touch!"

We are probably all familiar with the restaurant / bar type businesses that have automatic texts sending the latest coupons or deals- Tuesday happy hours, Five for Four Fridays and other specials. It's now become more common with other types of businesses including medical/dental practices. Once your audience provides their mobile phone number, don't be afraid to send out texts once or twice a month. Make sure the texts are useful, and don't send them more than once or twice per month; that could start to feel like spam for them. Texts are read over 90% of the time once received as opposed to emails, which are read only 17-20% of the time. A well-placed, well-timed text or two every now and then can really help drum up some business and get some clients to call you!

Direct Voicemail

Direct voicemail is the practice of sending a voicemail directly to the phone without the phone ever ringing; this is possible to do now with mobile phone voicemail systems, and in actuality it works very well. These systems are quite nifty; you can set up outbound voicemails that talk about something new or something local that you and your business did. The voicemail can be about thirty to ninety seconds, and instead of calling you can send it directly to their phone. The voicemail notifier pops up but the phone never rings, meaning the client can see the voicemail message and listen whenever they want. It's non-intrusive and as a result the listen rate is much higher.

This is one of the reasons we recommended earlier to get mobile phone numbers from each of your lead sources. It not only opens up texting as a marketing channel, but the direct voicemail tactic as well. Voicemail is very personal and very effective, and it's best used for events or other local initiatives your practice may be doing. An example might be seminars- if your business does seminars in the area about your topic, dropping a direct voicemail to each of your clients is a great, personal way to let them know about your upcoming seminars. It's easy, non-intrusive, and works very well!

Summing Up

We called this chapter the "What's next?" chapter for a reason; many of these technologies are going to or are already beginning to affect the Internet marketing arena. In fact, some of these ideas and strategies that we've talked about are already coming into play. We've begun to experiment with these things with some of our clients who are ahead of the curve or are battling in very competitive markets, which illustrates that these ideas are not simply theory or fluff. They're real strategies that are beginning to come into the market, and it's a good idea to keep abreast of them going forward.

Talk to the provider that you're working with and see what their ideas are on each of these strategies. It's also important that you find the right provider, one who specializes in these techniques. Don't confuse website building with online marketing. The skill set is quite different. For more help, be sure to visit our website, www.breakthroughstrategies.co

Just the Facts:

- Mobile and social media are going to be the driving forces in marketing going forward: each are driving marketing to be more location-oriented, due to the always-on nature that combines and unites mobile and social. Keep up to date on each and don't miss any opportunities to be creative and capitalize on these markets!

- People give much stronger weight to opinions from friends: make sure you have a strong social presence, and leverage that social presence by having a well-established business that ranks high.

- Direct mailing still has a place in the world, but it should be driving clients to go to your website in order to get that warm lead and—more importantly—get them to use a channel that's more easily tracked and analyzed.

- Don't become complacent: Create new ways to innovate and incorporate new technologies, and make sure to work with service providers that are online marketing experts and can help you create a robust and profitable online marketing machine

CHAPTER ELEVEN
HOW TO GET HELP GETTING ALL OF THIS DONE

How to Find People to do this for you

The most important member of your team may be the person or company that can implement, optimize and systemize each of the areas discussed in this book.   Let's face it, you didn't go to school, pass whatever licensing is required, and build your practice just so you could spend 11 non-billable hours a day uploading videos, submitting listings to directories, and designing websites.

Now we really wish we had better news for you, but finding competent people to do this work for you is not easy. Most web designers are broke, they know very little about marketing.   This is not the person you can trust with your marketing budget so be thorough in deciding who to invest with.

We're asked all the time where to find a good web person. And our answer is that every time we find one who knows what they are doing (they are rare), we hire them to work on our team. Of course, joking aside, the alternatives, like outsourcing this work to India or to some fly-by-night business will cause more work than it will save.

And having one of your front office team members or assistants do this work will drive you both crazy and possibly ruin your practice.

So How Can I Get All Of This Done?

We trust by now you'll agree, local web marketing is probably the most time-sensitive, urgent issue on your practice calendar right now. It may not seem like it at the moment, but when you review this book later on, you may wish you had a time machine to get you back to this day.

The local Internet marketing door is WIDE open right now, but it is closing fast...and we would not want you to miss out on future growth just because you had little or no time on your hands.

It's also very difficult to find good people to help you with this. Most web designers don't have the training in marketing. Outsourcing this kind of work to India or elsewhere is potentially hazardous to your practice.

In the interest of full disclosure, we provide a turn-key, 100% Done-For-You service which means you send us your business contact information and we do the rest. It's literally ALL done for you.   Unfortunately for

some potential clients we had to turn away, we restrict ourselves to only

one practice area in any given geographical area. We can't help both you

and your local competitors achieve first page ranking. Makes sense

doesn't it?

Having said all of that, if you feel that you are a business that we should

choose to work with and you would like to find out about my team's

availability to help you and to get all of this DONE FOR YOU, please

contact us at...

Phone: (407) 545-7794
Email: info@breakthroughstrategies.co
Web: www.breakthroughstrategies.co

We will, at the very least, be able to tell you if we are already working

with your practice type.

If we decide to move forward with you, we always start with a Web

Strategy Diagnosis. This just begins the discussion as to how we possibly

work together. And while we know that some people take this

experience-backed, high-quality web strategy then go and hire a cheap

local marketing agency, we also know that the best customers, those who understand the value of growing their business by maximizing their online marketing investment will ask us to just do it for them. We are looking for a small number of clients to build a long-term relationship with. And if that sounds like your business, then please feel free to write or call.

You've reached the end of this book, but you certainly haven't reached the end of how we can help you. If you've followed all the techniques and processes in this book and really took it to heart, you're well prepared to ratchet up your online marketing.

APPENDIX A: GLOSSARY

ANALYTICS: Analytics are technical measures you can take to see what happens with visitors on your website: how long they stay, what they click, how many of them return to the website, and statistics of that nature. One of the best analytic software packages out there currently is Google Analytics, which is also free.

AUTO-RESPONDER: An auto-responder is a system put in place to automatically respond to communication initiated by a potential client, usually via email. Auto-responders can range from simple to extremely complex, and can either send just one generic email or choose from dozens of templates depending on the form used by the potential client or the information provided to the auto-responder by the potential client.

BING: A major search engine, like Google and Yahoo. It has many of the same features and has the next-largest market share of any of the search engines, after Google.

BLOG: Originally an abbreviation of the term "web log", it has now come to mean a type of website (or part of a website) that is frequently updated with new content and has many interactive options for users to leave comments and otherwise participate; many blogs are powered by software explicitly designed to make this frequent updating an easier and smoother process, like Wordpress or Typepad.

CALL TO ACTION: Content on a website or other method of communication that appeal to the reader to contact the business.

CRM: An acronym for "Customer Relationship Management". In the context of Internet marketing, it most often refers to the software put in place that manages clients and potential clients of the business; names, locations, likes, dislikes, needs, and other information that the business may find relevant.

DIRECTORY: In the sense of Internet marketing, a website or part of a website whose purpose is to list businesses. Many of these, like Yelp, Merchant Circle, or CitySearch, also contain reviews of businesses that are often user-generated and submitted.

DUPLICATE CONTENT: Identical content that appears on multiple websites. Search engines have created ways of detecting this and often have algorithms that even detect if the content has just been altered slightly; content that has just be altered slightly and is still virtually identical to the original content will still be flagged as duplicate content by many search engines.

E-COMMERCE: The buying and selling of products and services over the Internet.

FACEBOOK: A social networking site that is currently the most popular in the world; it allows users to network with each other and socialize, including sharing photos, thoughts, status updates, and wall posts with each other.

FACEBOOK PLACES: A specific segment of the social networking site Facebook that allows users to see local spots around them as well as update their location in real-time from mobile phones or other means, allowing other users to see where they are at any given time.

GEOLOCATION: In Internet marketing and SEO, a term used to describe location-specific information; normally city and state for most local businesses.

GOOGLE MAPS: A part of Google's website that primarily deals with maps and navigation. One of the features of Google Maps is the ability for local businesses to list themselves on it, and the local search return feature was originally a part of this system. Google later integrated it into the main search system when it proved to be popular.

GOOGLE PLACES / GOOGLE + LOCAL: A part of Google's website that allows a business to have a specific page dedicated to them. It often hooks in with their location on Google Maps, and it features user-generated reviews of the business as well as links to other directories and review sites.

IP ADDRESS: A unique number that identifies a computer on a network.

KEYWORD: A term that a user searches against in a search engine to retrieve content that contains or is relevant to the term.

KEYWORD DENSITY: The use of a specific keyword present in any given piece of content. For example, given the keyword "racing" used five times in a 500-word blog post, the keyword density of "racing" would be 1%. Optimal keyword density is between 3 and 4%, and should not exceed 4% or it may be flagged as spamming.

KEYWORD PHRASE / LONG TAIL KEYWORD PHRASE: A phrase comprised of individual words but treated like a single keyword for the purposes of a search, like "NASCAR car racing" or "racing opportunities in Texas".

KEYWORD RICH: Content that has many keywords and uses them often, with good keyword density.

KEYWORD TOOL: Tools created to help select optimal keywords for search engine marketing, like Google's Keyword Tool. They often contain information such as amount of searches for a particular keyword and other metrics that help ascertain how popular or prevalent a given keyword or keyword phrase may be.

LINKEDIN: A social networking site that is geared towards businesses and professionals, enabling them to link up and network more effectively.

LOCAL SEARCH RETURN: A feature within Google's search engine that returns location-specific results for a user who types in keywords that relate to local businesses. A map and local businesses that are relevant to the search result would appear in the ensuing search page.

NICHING: The practice of specializing your marketing strategy to a certain keyword or keyword phrase in order to rank in the highest spot in a local search return for that keyword or keyword phrase.

ROI: An acronym for "Return on Investment," which means the amount of profit; in literal terms, the amount of money returned for the amount of money invested.

SEARCH ALGORITHM: A series of computer algorithms used by major search engines to index, search, and rank websites on the Internet.

SEARCH ENGINE: A website or company, like Google, Bing, or Yahoo, that indexes other websites on the Internet and allows users to enter keywords in order to find relevant websites.

SEO: An acronym for "Search Engine Optimization." It refers to the section of marketing that tries to increase exposure and clientele by using techniques and strategies to rank high on Internet search engines. Often interchanged with SEM (Search Engine Marketing).

SOCIAL MEDIA: Sites whose primary purpose is to enable users to share content with each other and socialize on the Internet; examples of websites that fall into this category are Facebook, Twitter, and LinkedIn.

SPAM: In Internet parlance, spam was originally used to refer to any unsolicited bulk messages sent over email. It is now also commonly used to refer to content on the Internet which is not useful and designed to make a page rank higher on search engines by tricking search engine algorithms into rating the content as more useful than it actually is.

TWEET: An individual post on Twitter.

TWITTER: A social networking service that allows users to post 140-character tweets to their account, with the ability for other users to follow them and respond to the tweets.

UNIQUE SELLING POSITION (USP): Unique Selling Position separates you from your competition in a specific market place. The term is often used to refer to any aspect of an object that differentiates it from similar objects.

URL: An acronym for "Uniform Resource Locator". It is the name that the user types into the browser bar in order to access a specific website; for example, "www.google.com" or "www.bing.com" would be examples of URLs.

ABOUT THE AUTHOR

MIKE LIGUORI

CEO & Chief Strategist – Breakthrough Strategies

"To lay waste a talent, a gift that's uniquely yours… by not sharing it with the world is an insidious thing to consider"   Mike Liguori

BIOGRAPHY

The greatest skill we can develop is to ask great questions. When we do, not only do we demand great answers, but an unbelievable world opens for us.

Mike Liguori is a provocative thought leader focused on facilitating peak performance in the individual and in company/corporate cultures. A deep financial background combined with sales and marketing excellence, thorough leadership training and an avid curiosity for tracking and measuring human potential provide the backdrop for every relationship. Mike is focused on continuous growth and contribution and challenges every relationship to be the best it can be.

Mike has over 20 years of experience developing businesses and their leaders in organizations as diverse as Business Breakthroughs International with Tony Robbins and Chet Holmes, Private Asset Group and his own former brand the CPA Financial Alliance. Mike is also affiliated with Robert G Allen and the Fortune in You Company.

In his role with Breakthrough Strategies, Liguori works tirelessly to bring clients and audiences face-to-face with the next breakthrough – an incredibly passionate, fully resourceful, and totally energized and on fire change agent!!!

"I Re-introduce you to YOU… the one you always knew was there. Far too many people focus singularly on the critical voice in their head and critical voices around them. They settle for way less than their true potential." Mike says. "Each of us have the same opportunity to change the world... and far too many of us get cut off from our source and settle for a mere fraction of what we're capable of".

Both a Business and Life Coach as well as Speaker, Liguori counsels Entrepreneurs, Info-Preneurs, Creative Types and Business Leaders that seek greater success, achievement, fulfillment and leadership skills in every area of their life.

Liguori adds, "One of the greatest lessons I've learned is that leadership is a mind thing. The past doesn't equal the future, or the present. I don't care if you're a janitor or if you're a CEO...When you show up with intention, with focus, with the power to anticipate and the power to influence.... This is my definition of a true leader. There's no difference between these two individuals. I can tell you that person won't be scrubbing toilets for long with that mindset."

He began his career as a CPA and recognized early on that numbers matter, but not as much as people. So his focus moved quickly on to leadership development. Instead of asking "where have you been," his emphasis migrated first to "where do you want to go" and finally to "who do you want to be?" Mike spent much of his early career building a successful consulting/CPA practice. The practice and his continued philosophy focused on developing each of the major impact areas that affect the organization – not just financial results. Mike is also an avid real estate investor as well as a committed serial entrepreneur.

"My passion is in growing and asking "how may I serve". I'm an avid reader and I love and excel at helping myself and others achieve peak performance." He lives in Central Florida and enjoys writing and playing music and working out and living/eating healthy! Mike is celebrating 25 years with his lovely wife and partner Veronica. He has a beautiful daughter a brand new grandson, Logan Michael.

BRING US TO SPEAK AT YOUR NEXT EVENT:

Want to bring the author to speak at your next event?

Our programs are designed to optimize online marketing strategies. We focus on advanced SEO (Search Engine Optimization) and Local Search as an alternative means to traditional marketing, as well as business growth through coaching and training on process improvement.

Our Programs: We offer several different programs including:

1) Websites, Google, and More: Getting Clients Online the Ethics, Pitfalls, and Techniques

2) Turning Clicks Into Clients: The Ultimate Presentation for Online Marketing

3) Social Media and Your Company: How to Leverage and Convert Clicks Into New Clients With Facebook, Twitter, Linkedin, and Google+

This list changes from time-to-time depending on technology and demand. For a complete list of topics please contact us at info@breakthroughstrategies.co or (407) 545-7794

BONUS!

Discover Exactly How You Can Make a Few Slight Adjustments and Begin to Dominate Local Search…It All Starts with Your 22 Point Review.

http://videomarketing.breakthroughstrategies.co/downloads/exponential-growth-planner/

If you want our valuable Web Strategy Diagnosis and Audit, visit this link. There is no obligation on either your or our part. This just begins the discussion as to how we may be able to help you. This URL gives you a valuable discount (as a reader and fan) It's a great opportunity to get your online presence reviewed.

And while we know that some people take this experience-backed, high-quality web strategy then go and hire a cheap local marketing agency, we also know that the best customers, those who understand the value of growing their business by maximizing their online marketing investment will ask us to just do it for them. We are always interested in beginning a dialog with high quality clients that we can build a long term relationship with. If this sounds like you, then please feel free to email or call.

Phone: (407) 545-7794

Email: info@breakthroughstrategies.co

www.ingramcontent.com/pod-product-compliance
Lightning Source LLC
Chambersburg PA
CBHW041314210326
41599CB00008B/264